THE
WHITE
HOUSE

Edited by

Frank Freidel ▪ı William Pencak

THE

WHITE

HOUSE

The First Two Hundred Years

BOSTON

NORTHEASTERN UNIVERSITY PRESS

Northeastern University Press

Copyright 1994 The White House Historical Association

The publication of this volume has been supported
in part by a grant from the National
Endowment for the Humanities.

Library of Congress Cataloging-in-Publication Data

The White House : the first two hundred years / edited by
Frank Freidel, William Pencak.
p. cm.
Includes bibliographical references (p.) and index.
ISBN 1-55553-170-9 (cl. : acid-free)
1. White House (Washington, D.C.) 2. Presidents—United States.
3. Washington (D.C.)—Social life and customs. 4. Washington (D.C.)
—Buildings, structures, etc. I. Freidel, Frank Burt.
II. Pencak, William, 1951– .
F204.W5W65 1994
975.3—dc20 93-31360

Designed by David Ford

Composed in Trump Medieval by Coghill Composition,
Inc., Richmond, Virginia. Printed and bound by The Maple Press,
York, Pennsylvania. The paper is
Sebago Eggshell, an acid-free sheet.

MANUFACTURED IN THE UNITED STATES OF AMERICA
98 97 96 95 94   5 4 3 2 1

This book is dedicated to the many men and women, both past and present, who have worked at the White House and whose loving care of the building and grounds has preserved this national treasure for all Americans.

■ı

IN MEMORY

FRANK FREIDEL (1916–1993) achieved unusual distinction as a scholar, a teacher, and a human being. A pioneer in the study of Franklin D. Roosevelt, he made himself a leading authority on Roosevelt's political career. He assisted in planning the symposium at which these papers were presented; he graciously agreed to edit this book and up to a few days before his death hoped that he would be able to complete that task. Those who were fortunate enough to know him will miss Frank.

Contents

viii ■| Contents

List of Illustrations

List of Contributors

DANIEL J. BOORSTIN, historian and public servant, directed the Library of Congress from 1975 until 1987. Author of *The Creators* and *The Discoverers*, his trilogy, *The Americans*, was awarded the Bancroft, the Parkman, and the Pulitzer prizes. In 1990 he received the National Book Award for his lifetime contribution to literature. His books have been translated into more than twenty languages.

BETTY BOYD CAROLI is Professor of History at the City University of New York. She is the author of *Italian Repatriation from the United States, Today's Immigrants: Their Stories* (with Thomas Kessner), *Immigrants Who Returned Home, First Ladies*, and *Inside the White House: A Pictorial History of the First Two Hundred Years*.

JOHN MILTON COOPER, JR., is William Francis Allen Professor of History at the University of Wisconsin. His most recent books are *The Warrior and the Priest: Woodrow Wilson and Theodore Roosevelt* and *Pivotal Decades: The United States, 1900–1920*.

DAVID HERBERT DONALD is Charles Warren Professor Emeritus at Harvard University. He is the author of *Lincoln Reconsidered, Divided We Fought*, and *Charles Sumner and the Coming of the Civil War*. He has twice won the Pulitzer Prize.

ROBERT H. FERRELL is Professor Emeritus of History at Indiana University. He has published widely on the presidency, including *Woodrow*

Wilson and World War I, Harry S. Truman and the Modern American Presidency, The Eisenhower Diaries, and, most recently, *Ill-Advised: Presidential Health and Public Trust.*

ELISE K. KIRK is the author of *Musical Highlights from the White House.* Currently, she teaches music history at Catholic University of America and lectures at the John F. Kennedy Center for the Performing Arts. Her most recent awards are from the Hoover Presidential Library Association and the American Society of Composers.

DAVID MCCULLOUGH is known to millions of Americans as the host of the award-winning PBS series "The American Experience" and the narrator of such television documentaries as "The Civil War" and "LBJ." He is the author of *The Johnstown Flood, The Great Bridge, The Path Between the Seas, Mornings on Horseback, Brave Companions,* and *Truman.* His most recent award is the Pulitzer Prize, and he has twice received the National Book Award as well as the Parkman Prize, the Samuel Eliot Morison Award, and the Cornelius Ryan Award.

GEORGE E. REEDY is Emeritus Professor of Journalism at Marquette University. He is former Press Secretary of the White House and Special Assistant to the President (Lyndon B. Johnson) and former Staff Director of the U.S. Senate Democratic Policy Committee. His books include *The Twilight of the Presidency, The Presidency in Flux, The U.S. Senate: Paralysis or Search for Consensus, Lyndon B. Johnson: A Memoir, The Twilight of the Presidency: From Johnson to Reagan,* and *From the Ward to the White House: The Irish in American Politics.*

ROBERT V. REMINI is Professor of History Emeritus and Research Professor of Humanities Emeritus at the University of Illinois at Chicago. His most recent books include *Henry Clay: Statesman for the Union* and *The Life of Andrew Jackson.* He is currently writing a biography of Daniel Webster.

EUGENE L. ROBERTS, JR., is Professor of Journalism at the University of Maryland. He was for eighteen years editor of the *Philadelphia In-*

quirer. Previously, he had been national editor, chief civil rights correspondent, and chief Vietnam correspondent for the *New York Times.*

RICHARD NORTON SMITH is Director of the Herbert Hoover Presidential Library in West Branch, Iowa, and is former Acting Director of the Dwight D. Eisenhower Center in Abilene, Kansas. He is the author of numerous books, including biographies of Thomas E. Dewey and Herbert Hoover. His most recent work, *Patriarch: George Washington and the New American Nation,* was selected by the Book-of-the-Month Club and the History Book Club. He is now researching a biography of Colonel Robert R. McCormick.

DOUGLAS B. WARD is a doctoral candidate in the Department of Journalism and teaches at the University of Maryland. He has worked as an editor at several newspapers, including the *Philadelphia Inquirer,* the *Philadelphia Daily News,* and the *Kansas City Times.*

EDWIN M. YODER, JR., is Professor of Journalism and Humanities at Washington and Lee University and writes a syndicated column for the Washington Post Writers Group. He was awarded a Pulitzer Prize for editorial writing while working at the *Washington Star* and he was editorial-page editor of the *Greensboro* (N.C.) *Daily News.*

Preface

President George Washington's vision for the home and office of the chief executive of the United States was embodied in the design for the White House by architect James Hoban. On October 13, 1792, the ceremonial cornerstone of the President's House was set in place. Two hundred years of history at the White House have transpired since then, during which time the White House has been transformed into a powerful national institution while retaining its original functions.

To observe the significance of the White House as the home and office of the president of the United States and as a symbol of American democracy recognized worldwide, a series of public programs were presented in Washington, D.C., and across the country throughout 1992. The commemorative programs and activities provided Americans, both young and old, with a better understanding and appreciation of the importance of the White House and the role it has played in our nation's history.

A symposium sponsored by the White House Historical Association and the National Park Service was held October 13–15, 1992, in Washington, D.C. Distinguished scholars who spoke at that event have given freely of their time and talent to create the contents of this book. We gratefully acknowledge the financial support provided by the White House Historical Association and the National Endowment for the Humanities for the symposium and this publication. Special thanks are extended to William A. Frohlich, Director of the Northeastern University Press, for his encouragement and support of this publication. Frank Freidel's enthusiasm for this book will always be remembered. Mr. Freidel and his colleague William Pencak also provided valuable editorial guidance. Finally, Bernard R. Meyer, Executive Vice President, White House Historical Association, and Charles E. Fisher, Historian, National Park Service, were instrumental in making this publication possible.

REX W. SCOUTEN
Curator, The White House

GARY J. WALTERS
Chief Usher, The White House

Introduction

Just as the American presidency is a unique office, so is the residence of the holder of that office. Unlike the chief executives of nearly every other free country, the president of the United States serves as both head of state and head of government. Of the major powers, only France, and only during the last three and a half decades under the Fifth Republic, has combined these functions to some extent, and not so thoroughly as in America. As a result, the President's House, as the mansion was formally called during its first hundred years, has always had a dual personality. It is as if a single edifice in London played the roles of both Buckingham Palace and Number 10 Downing Street, with Windsor Castle thrown in as well, for openness to the public. How then might it be possible to commemorate and, more important, to understand the varied functions and aspects of this unique place over a span of two centuries?

That was the task faced by the White House Historical Association in planning for the two hundredth anniversary of the laying of the cornerstone of the building, which took place on October 13, 1792. For three years, starting in the summer of 1989, a group of scholars, journalists, and public servants met to address this multifaceted assignment. The fruit of their labors was a symposium held in Washington from October 13 to 15, 1992, and a variety of events, including a reception in the White House on the day of the two-hundredth anniversary hosted by President and Mrs. Bush. The bulk of the symposium consisted of presentations and discussions about the multiple and changing roles of the White House. From those sessions, twelve papers have been selected to illustrate the scope of the subject, especially public aspects of life in and surrounding this building. One of the symposium's planners and participants, Frank M. Freidel, a leading American historian and biographer of Franklin D. Roosevelt, began to edit these papers for this volume, but, tragically, he died in January 1993, before he could complete the work. It fell to William Pencak to complete the editing and to me to write these introductory words.

These essays stand separately as insightful contributions to specific topics, but they also come together to offer a kaleidoscopic view of a two-hundred-year-old public institution. Far be it from me to try to add to the stories and reflections provided by these distinguished contributors. Rather, let me simply preview some common threads that run through these essays.

In the opening essay, Daniel Boorstin compares the White House not just with familiar European palaces and government buildings, but also with the Alhambra. He does this to make the important point that a nation's architecture finds reflection in its public rituals. As he observes, in contrast to those famed Old World edifices, this New World offspring of democracy and mutability has had to embody "accessibility, civility, and representativeness." Hence the White House has assumed the simultaneous guises of ceremonial stage, ministerial office, and home to a rotating tenantry.

This assumption of multiple functions did not happen either swiftly or smoothly, as Robert Remini points out in his account of the house's early years. Besides having a defeated lame duck for its first resident in 1800, the building was burned down by the British in 1814, rebuilt and reopened in 1817, and all through these years subjected to recurrent criticisms of its occupants' European tastes in furnishing and excessive spending. Interestingly, the name "White House" seems to have come into wider use around the time of the building's destruction in 1814, although this did not become its official title until Theodore Roosevelt so decreed in 1901, after a century of nearly continuous occupancy.

The first Roosevelt also coined the term "bully pulpit" to define and expand the presidency. As Richard Norton Smith demonstrates, he made the White House into the public platform that it has remained for succeeding presidents. Such an achievement required both inward- and outward-looking efforts. Under Theodore Roosevelt, the building and grounds underwent renovation and restoration to reaffirm their "colonial appearance and austere traditions." Meanwhile, Roosevelt and his successors constantly adapted the house to accommodate the growing power and publicity of their office. Increasingly, chief executives devoted themselves and their dwelling to the care, feeding, and — to be honest — manipulation of what are now called "the media."

Even before those changes occurred, however, one president had lived in a storm center in the White House. This was Abraham Lincoln, who, as David Herbert Donald shows, endured the sharpest public and private tribulations of any occupant. Other presidents have had to lead the country in war, but only Lincoln had to fight at home against his fellow Americans to ensure the nation's survival and to eradicate slavery. All the while, he and his family bore the burdens of social ostracism, continuous civilian and military visitors, his wife's compulsive spending habits, their son's death, and finally his own assassination at the moment of victory. The Lincoln saga made the White House a tragic setting to match Oedipus's Theban abode or Hamlet's Elsinore.

Of the eight presidents who have died in office, only the first two, William Henry Harrison and Zachary Taylor, drew their last breath in the White House. More often, both assassins' bullets and mortal illnesses have felled chief executives while they were away from their temporary home. On at least three occasions, however, the White House has served as a refuge for a disabled president. In the summer of 1881, James Garfield lay for two months inside the mansion suffering from the gunshot wound that finally claimed his life at a New Jersey summer resort. Not quite forty years later, Woodrow Wilson became an invalid after suffering a stroke in October 1919, and he seldom ventured outside the grounds or even the walls of the White House between then and the end of his presidency in March 1921. From 1933 to 1945, Franklin Roosevelt's inability to walk remained largely concealed from public view within the confines of the building, as did his suffering from severe hypertension during the last year and a half of his life. My essay examines the Wilson episode because it presents the clearest case of presidential disability in American history and the weightiest public consequences of such disability.

Wilson's disability, and perhaps Roosevelt's also, caused serious consequences because, as the United States grew in size, wealth, and global reach, so too did the government need to run a twentieth-century colossus. As Robert Ferrell recounts, the White House physically mirrored that expansion. By the time Theodore Roosevelt finished his tenure, an office complex had sprouted on the West Wing, with William Howard Taft being the first to occupy the Oval Office. That room acquired its present location under the second Roosevelt, whose presidency also occasioned the use of a portion of the adjoining Victorian structure now known as the Executive Office Building. That building's previous occupants, the Departments of State, War, and the Navy, now require no less than Foggy Bottom and the Pentagon to hold them.

Size and power exacted a stiff price in accessibility. Before the First World War, the White House stood open to anyone who wanted to drop in. Until the Second World War, clearance to enter was easy to obtain. But in the latter half of this century, national security and, as Eugene Roberts and Douglas Ward show, the desires of radicals and reformers to petition and protest have combined to restrict access to accredited journalists and to channel public demonstrations into special procedures. No more than twenty-five persons at a time may picket in front of the Pennsylvania Avenue entrance without a special permit: 128 such permits were issued during the first nine months of 1992.

Handling the press has grown into one of the biggest demands on space and staff in the White House. That was not always the case, as George Reedy observes. Through the 1920s, major newspapers concentrated on covering Congress, usually almost exclusively from local angles. The White House became a significant reporters' beat only in Franklin Roosevelt's time. Since then, especially after the advent of television, a sharp divergence in function has grown up between the more strictly journalistic tasks of the press secretary and the public relations functions of the communications director.

Those changes have unquestionably enhanced the visibility and impact of the "bully pulpit" at 1600 Pennsylvania Avenue. But, as Edwin Yoder suggests, political profit does not automatically accrue to the occupant. Skill and attentiveness in exploiting opportunities have grown steadily more important, but so, it seems, has luck, without which even the greatest of communicators can still wind up looking like the Wizard of Oz.

Whether or not the White House ever really becomes a home to its fixed-term leaseholders, it has been the domicile of married partners for all but a decade and a half of its nearly two centuries of occupancy. As Betty Boyd Caroli relates, the role of presidential spouse has evolved with time, technology, and the demands of her husband's office. Jacqueline Kennedy thought the term "First Lady" would serve better as the name of a horse, but she both filled and augmented the four-part requirements of the modern First Lady as campaigner, communicator, promoter of programs, and curator of the White House.

Mrs. Kennedy is remembered not only for redecorating the house's public rooms, but for her patronage of the arts, most vividly symbolized by her invitation to the great cellist Pablo Casals to perform in the East Room. As Elise Kirk points out, Casals had played there six decades earlier at the invitation of the Roosevelts, as part of a tradition of presidential sponsorship and enjoyment of music that dates back to the White House's first occupants. The United States Marine Band played at a New Year's reception given by the Adamses in 1801; they played again at the two-hundredth anniversary reception on October 13, 1992.

This large house on a small rise of land, nestled amid trees and shrubs and flowers, not far from the river that, for four years, divided two warring nations, remains to invite other people in the future to its uses and enjoyments, as David McCullough shows in the concluding essay.

These essays do not exhaust the material covered at the two hundredth anniversary symposium. Architecture, art, decoration, and food were among other topics included. During the summer of 1992, an oral history session by former staff members recounted much about "downstairs" life at the White House, particularly its role in Washington's African-American community. But much was not covered. Time and space threw up unavoidable limits. Even more study of many aspects of this structure and its denizens awaits future inquirers. This symposium and these essays offer an invitation toward further appreciation of this great historic place with the plain name, the White House.

February 22, 1993   JOHN MILTON COOPER, JR.

THE
WHITE
HOUSE

Chapter

1

Roles of the President's House

Daniel J. Boorstin

You have asked me to try to put our White House in a wide historical perspective, and to suggest what the White House may tell us of large and characteristic features of our American democracy. I am charged, then, with reminding us even of the significant obvious, which we sometimes notice but often forget.

Democracies — and especially ours in the United States — despite their many strengths, are conspicuously weak in ritual. Yet ritual — a public ceremonial affirmation of community — satisfies a need felt in all societies. In our U.S.A. the only ritual required by our Constitution is the president's inauguration. It suggests the special aura, a democratic aura, that surrounds our president. And as it surrounds his inauguration, his ceremonial entering on his duties as the only public servant selected by the whole citizenry, so, too, it surrounds his residence.

Time alone is the resource that can enrich ritual and give it meaning. Yet this is one resource in which we in the U.S.A. are not especially rich.

In our democratic New World society, architecture can and does play the role of ritual. It can do this because architecture has many of the features of ritual:

1. It is structured.

2. It can be dramatic.

3. It provides a repetitive experience that ties us to
   the past.

4. It is communal, emphasizing and embodying the
   relation of people to one another and to their common past.

5. It is capable of embellishment, renewal, and subtle
   change.

6. It is durable and can outlive the generations.

Architecture, too, has the advantage over ritual in not requiring a priest-
hood or even a leading human performer to make its impact. Its separation from any individual affirms the prime importance of the community and the product over the interests of any one leader or generation.
Also, by contrast with ritual, it suggests and affirms the *material* foundations of community.

In some conspicuous ways our distinctive history has given an especially revealing role to our architecture. American mobility, for example, was vividly embodied in our first characteristic domestic architecture. This was not the log cabin, which was a New World version of an
older Swedish design. It was the balloon frame house. An American con-
trivance, quickly built and quickly demounted for removal to some distant place, the balloon frame house was invented in our West for impa-
tient and ambitious Americans who might want to move from Chicago
to Omaha and beyond. It first appeared prominently in Chicago in 1833
and would continue to serve American needs for speedy construction by
people who lacked the Old World mortise-and-tenon skills of cabinet-
maker, joiner, or carpenter. It was destined to become the pioneering
design for American suburbia.

In these western communities of transients and boosters, architecture
also provided prominent symbols of community pride, rivalry, hospitality, and expansiveness. The hotel was one of the most distinctive and
remarkable of these American architectural symbols, marking the birth
and optimistic spirit of newly founded cities across the continent. The
hotel was complemented by other speedily built monuments to the
pride of new communities — county courthouses and grandiose state

The President's House as originally built. Courtesy of the White House.

capitols. Then, in the later nineteenth century, catastrophe (like the Chicago fire of 1871) and commercial opportunity led American businessmen to create peculiarly American "cathedrals of commerce," better known as skyscrapers. These became symbols of the boundless heavenward aspiration of a technologically inspired democratic nation.

But architecture also has had a political significance and symbolism, which was brilliantly illustrated in Great Britain during World War II in the too-little-celebrated observations of the prophetic Winston Churchill. After a German bomb destroyed the House of Commons on May 10, 1941, the members debated the question of how to rebuild. The House was oblong in shape, and some suggested that it be rebuilt in a semicircular form. To this Churchill strenuously objected. He stood firm for the original oblong in which it had been constructed after the fire of 1834.

As usual, Churchill's reasons were interesting and based on broad principles. He explained that it was because he favored the party system of government (as against what he called the "group" system). In a semicircular chamber, he explained, "it is easy for an individual to move through those insensible gradations from left to right, but the act of crossing the floor [of a rectangular chamber] is one which requires serious consideration."

Churchill also urged that the new building not be too large, for, he said, "a small chamber and a sense of intimacy are indispensable." Surprisingly, Churchill even insisted that the reconstructed House of Commons building "should not be big enough to contain all its members at once without overcrowding, and that there should be no question of every Member having a separate seat reserved for him." Otherwise, he said, nine-tenths of the time the debates would be "in the depressing atmosphere of an almost empty or half-empty chamber." All this was necessary to preserve the traditional atmosphere of the House which "has lifted our affairs above the mechanical sphere into the human sphere." This is an observation that we too may fairly make of our White House.

In any event, Churchill urged, it was crucial that the House of Commons be rebuilt as soon as possible — on old foundations and in the old dimensions. There must be no danger of the House not having its place of meeting. "I rank the House of Commons," he declared, " — the most powerful Assembly in the whole world — at least as important as a fortification or a battleship even in time of war." Churchill's irresistible eloquence persuaded his colleagues that only such a building would give the public business of the Parliament "a sense of Crowd and Urgency." The ever-fluent Churchill ended his speech by thanking the House of Lords for letting the Commons meet in their "spacious, splendid hall . . . under this gilded, ornamented, statue-bedecked roof." And it is interesting for our present purposes that he concluded:

> Mid pleasures and palaces though we may roam,
> Be it ever so humble, there's no place like home.

We surely would not want the residence of our president to convey what Churchill wanted for the House of Commons — "a sense of Crowd and Urgency." We would prefer a Sense of Intimacy and Informality. But we can say much more than that. For our White House, our President's House, like the House of Commons, has carried and can continue to carry some special meanings for our society and our government.

I was recently and vividly reminded of these special meanings when I visited another history-laden set of buildings that also long served as the residence of a head of state. It is, to my knowledge, the only other such public building that takes its name from its color. And by its stark contrasts it may help us understand the meanings of our White House.

The building that I found so redolent of contrasts is, as some of you may have suspected, the famous Red House or Alhambra. It is so called from the Arabic word for red, the color of the sun-dried bricks, made of fine gravel and clay, of its outer walls. Built on a hill on the outskirts of Granada in southern Spain, it served as official residence of the Nasrite kings of Granada for some 250 years — from about 1240 to 1492 — a half century longer than our White House has yet served as the residence of our presidents. And with its 2,000 servants and court officials, its staff only slightly exceeded the 1,767 employees (at latest count) in the Executive Office of the President (including 92 in the Executive Residence). Like our White House the Alhambra was a combination office and residence. Although the physical expanse of the Alhambra impresses us with its vast extent, the White House grounds are hardly meager, covering some eighteen acres.

Do not be outraged by this comparison of the works of an absolute Moorish potentate with those of our popularly elected, constitutionally limited president. This outlandish contrast of the roles of these two architectural metaphors helps us discover the distinctive roles of our White House. When I recently visited the exotic Alhambra's storied halls and walls and towers and gardens and enjoyed its exotic charms, it seemed to provide me a vivid and suggestive metaphor for what our White House is not. And so it can help me focus the significance of the building we celebrate and commemorate today. By contrast, the Alhambra brought into high relief three grand and simple features of our President's House as clues to our whole scheme of government.

Of these the most obvious and perhaps most American is *Accessibility*. The Alhambra, like other residences of rulers, is a palace in a castle. Old World rulers, needing protection from foreign invaders, rival princes, and discontented subjects, naturally ensconced themselves and their courts behind high walls and moats, securely defended from heavily fortified towers. A familiar example is Windsor Castle, a fortified royal residence from Saxon times (c. ninth century). The need for this protection is attested by the beautifully preserved filigreed royal palace in the Alhambra, buttressed by the massive walls and towers of the Alcazaba, the adjoining military quarters, several times destroyed and rebuilt. It is not surprising that uneasy absolute rulers should dwell in a fortress-palace.

Nor is it surprising that our elected president, living in a house that the citizens consider to be their gift and their property, should be at ease with his people and give them easy access to his home. Where else can a citizen go to his elected representative and secure a ticket allowing him to enter and tour the actual present residence of the head of state and government? Whenever I drive past the White House and see the lines of Americans of all ages and no special status waiting for their tour of the house they have provided for their elected chief public servant, I am reminded of how distinctive are our American institutions. Regal residences in other times and places have been closely guarded against the vulgar eyes and muddy feet of the populace.

A view of the Alhambra Palace from the towers of the Generalife. The town is at the right. The palace looks down on the city and dominates it. The beautiful Moorish art and courtyards are accessible only to those who are admitted inside. Courtesy of the Bettmann Archive.

But our White House is an emphatically public residence, which some of its tenants have discovered to their irritation. Presidents have reacted differently to the pains of living in a public facility. "It seems like there was always somebody for supper," President Truman complained. But while President Reagan commented that "you get a little stir crazy during the week," he also good-naturedly noted that the experience reminded him of his youth. "Now, here I am," he said, "sort of living above the store again." But some who never had the opportunity to live in the White House solaced themselves with its trials. So did General William T. Sherman in his often-quoted quip, "If forced to choose between the penitentiary and the White House for four years, I would say the penitentiary, thank you."

Another too easily forgotten feature embodied in our White House is *Civility*. Just as the deliberations of both houses of our Congress have been remarkably decorous — with none of the throwing of ink-bottles and screaming of epithets found in parliamentary bodies of some of the more civilized countries — so, despite rare lapses, our presidents have generally treated their opponents and have been treated by their opponents with restraint and decorum.

The Anglo-American poet W. H. Auden once observed that the most remarkable feature of an American presidential election is that on election night none of the candidates — win or lose — would be packing his baggage to leave the country. This is not a feature of presidential elections around the world. Civility has remained a robust American political tradition embodied in the conduct of presidential life in the White House.

I was reminded of this by a melodramatic tale of the Alhambra's history that for me provides an edifying if exotic contrast, which no visitor to the Alhambra is apt to forget. This tale attaches to one of the more picturesque rooms, the so-called Abencerrajes Gallery, leading on to the unsurpassed elegance of the famous Court of the Lions. Here, according to legend, the ruthless King Boabdil, sometime in the 1480s, summoned the thirty-six leaders of the rival Abencerrajes family for a peacemaking banquet. But he seized the occasion to dispose of them by beheading all thirty-six. He then tossed their heads into the central basin beneath the fantastic stalactite Moorish ceiling and its charming star-shaped lantern cupola. The red stains still visible in the central basin are said by some to come from the iron oxide in the marble, while others see in them the indelible bloody marks of the decapitated heads. Some historians attribute this bloody banquet not to Boabdil, but to his father, yet there remains substance to the story.

Despite the sometimes bitter rivalries of American party politics, the halls of the White House have remained quite unbloody. Burned by the British in 1814, it was rebuilt and extended in the next decade. Although we have suffered several assassinations of our presidents, none of these occurred in or even near the White House. The only notorious occasion of conspicuous disorder in the president's residence is the familiar inaugural reception for President Andrew Jackson in March 1829. Then, as William Seale vividly recounts in *The President's House*, Democracy came to the White House with a vengeance. The crowds surging into the oval drawing room pushed President Jackson against the wall until he gasped for breath. Some friends had the presence of mind to help him escape through a window onto the South Portico, then to the ground, and took him off to refuge where he had been staying, in Gadsby's hotel. The *Washington City Chronicle* blandly reported that "the President's hospitality on this occasion was in some measure misapplied." There was no loss of life, but considerable loss of "the dignity of the Presidency as well as the character of the nation." "But it was the People's day," one witness recorded, "and the People's President and the People would rule. . . . The noisy and disorderly rabble in the President's House brought to my mind descriptions I had read, of the mobs in the Tuileries and at Versailles." But there were no beheadings, no guillotine, and even this sort of mild disorder by thirsty Washingtonians would not be repeated. It became only another example of the distinctive openness of the president's residence in a democracy.

This unusual episode suggests still another continuing feature of the architectural symbolism of the White House. I have mentioned *Accessibility* and *Civility;* a third is *Representativeness.* Compared with the official residences of the famous heads of other great nations, the White House is a prosaic place. With his *Tales of the Alhambra* (1832), Washington Irving (1783–1859), sometimes called the first American author to acquire an international reputation, provided us with a minor American classic embroidering the history and legends of that famous Red House of kings. The chapters of that book, written mostly while he stayed in a room in the royal palace of the Alhambra, still evoke the poetic redolence of the buildings, the architecture, the decoration, and their history. Watching "the declining daylight upon this Moorish pile," wrote Irving, "I was led into a consideration of the light, elegant and voluptuous character prevalent throughout its internal architecture and to contrast it with the grand but gloomy solemnity of the Gothic edifices, reared by the Spanish conquerors. The very architecture thus bespeaks the opposite and irreconcilable natures of the two warlike peoples who so long battled for the mastery of the Peninsula." And Irving was similarly inspired when he viewed the Alhambra by moonlight. "I have sat by hours at my window, inhaling the sweetness of the garden and musing on the chequered fortunes of those whose history is dimly shadowed out in the elegant memorials around." Although the White House has now stood for the two centuries which we celebrate in our meeting in a literate city of countless authors in a world whose fortunes have been shaped by the inhabitants of the President's House, we have yet to see any counterpart to Irving's work. We know no "Tales of the White House." Nor are we apt to.

The reason is a prime feature of this distinctly American architectural metaphor, what I call its *Representativeness*. As our political system has been designed not to give power to men of charisma, but to allow the nation to be governed by elected representatives, our White House offers the nation a scene of a president and his family leading lives not dissimilar from our own. It is a prosaic prospect, but one that elevates us citizens by reminding us that our president leads a life essentially like ours, in surroundings not resplendent and sumptuous, but grand and comfortable. Some of the more discriminating tenants of the White House have noted the similarity of the President's House to everybody else's house. Jacqueline Kennedy, reflecting on the prospect of her family's move into the White House, observed, "It looks like it's been furnished by discount stores." After she had moved in, a perceptive reporter observed that "she changed the White House from a plastic to a crystal bowl."

The dignity and decorum of daily life in the President's House can be contagious. The features that conspicuously reach the citizenry remind us less of the grandeur than of the commonplaceness of the resident president's life — the affection for children and grandchildren and dogs, the Thanksgiving Dinner, the Christmas Tree, the family birthday parties. Not even Whitman could be inspired by its commonplaceness, and the White House remains our most prosaic national monument.

In expressing the openness of American public life — with a convenient office for the press, in a society with "Sunshine Laws" that allow all citizens the right to scrutinize government records — the White House, too, symbolizes a democratic refusal to distinguish between the public and the private. During the president's incumbency, we expect him to make the White House his *home,* his place of family living. A continual public view of the president's life in the White House is provided by the president's photographer. The work of the remarkable Yoichi Okamoto, for example, has provided the public with an unprecedented, copious, and comprehensive view of the life of a president. Reporters, too, have become integral members of the White House family, symbolized by the newly convenient facilities provided them in the White House press room, which one reporter recently described as "an adult day-care center."

Because our president is both Head of State and Head of Government, special symbolic demands were made on the White House planners. The siting of the house itself succeeded in expressing the more obvious distinctive features of our constitutional government. (This, again, is in contrast to the situation in Great Britain or France, where the head of state is a separate and ceremonial person.) When President Washington and Major Pierre-Charles L'Enfant (1754–1825) chose two commanding sites a mile and a half apart for the Houses of Congress in the Capitol and for the President's House, they dramatized the separation of legislative and executive powers found in the Constitution. In Philadelphia, where the federal government had been before the move to Washington, this dramatic symbolism had been lacking. There the Congress had been meeting next door to Independence Hall, only a few blocks from the President's House. After the president delivered an address to the Congress, the members walked or rode in rented coaches to the nearby house where the president was lodged. The occasion was not properly expressive either of the separation of powers or of the dignity of the occasion. The move to Washington gave L'Enfant his chance to plan a proper capital for the new nation for whose creation he had fought and been wounded as a volunteer engineer serving at his own expense. L'Enfant seized his assignment with imagination, energy, and every virtue except discretion. He refused to accept advice, and when he saw a house obstructing a street that he had planned, without any legal authority he simply tore it down. Unfortunately, it belonged to an influential citizen, and this, among other indiscretions, caused the termination of L'Enfant's services on February 27, 1792.

L'Enfant, born in Paris, had a vision of capitals influenced by his view of Versailles. The frustration of his hopes, too, would reveal the distinctive role of the President's House in a New World constitutional democracy. As White House historian William Seale has observed, L'Enfant had fixed on locating legislative and executive branches on two widely separated eminences. He probably designed Pennsylvania Avenue (having in mind the ceremonial processions of European monarchs along boulevards lined by their cheering subjects) as a long, grand avenue to give still more dignity and emphasis to the separation of president from Congress. L'Enfant must have imagined a procession of state coaches drawn by richly caparisoned horses, carrying an impressive array of dignitaries. But when the avenue had its first trial, after President Adams addressed a joint session of the Congress on November 22, 1800, the effect was not impressive. Members of Congress made their way laboriously to the new President's House through a sea of mud, in miscellaneous vehicles, mostly hacks hired off the streets. Later, Congress passed a law to pave a walkway from the Capitol to the President's House. But L'Enfant's imagined grand procession after the president's address to the joint meetings of Congress never took place. Still, L'Enfant's vision was not entirely unfulfilled, for the Grand Avenue — Pennsylvania Avenue — did become the memorable scene for dramatizing the one American political ritual, the inauguration of the president. Later generations would preserve their distinctive images of each inauguration by the spectacle on that avenue of incoming and outgoing presidents.

What is the future role of the White House in American life and culture? In my view, its role nowadays as a historic place and monument of our traditions is more significant than ever. And it becomes ever more necessary with every advance in our technology. For the new media of the last century have tended to dissolve our sense of place and of time. "Is it live or is it taped?" When and where? Fewer and fewer places and times preserve their uniqueness, as we are overwhelmed by photography, movies, television, videotapes, documentaries, and recorded messages.

The question today is: can the White House remain a place that reassures us by vivifying the ties of our democratic government to individual living people with all their weaknesses, their warmth and informality?

N O T E

Oleg Grabar, *The Alhambra* (Cambridge: Harvard University Press, 1978), and M. H. Port, ed., *The Houses of Parliament* (New Haven: Yale University Press, 1976), provide the information and illustrations permitting comparison of these edifices with the White House.

Chapter

Becoming a National Symbol:
The White House in the
Early Nineteenth Century

Robert V. Remini

In November 1800, Abigail Adams, the wife of President John Adams and the mother of President John Quincy Adams, took one look at her new home and, like any Adams worthy of his or her salt, pronounced a critical judgment. "I had much rather live in the house at Philadelphia," she complained to her elder sister. "Not one room or chamber is finished of the whole," she said. "It is habitable by fires in every part, thirteen of which we are obliged to keep daily, or sleep in wet & damp places."[1]

When the Adamses moved into the spanking new Executive Mansion in the capital city, very few of the thirty rooms had been plastered. There were no bells in the house to summon servants. Little firewood had been stockpiled; the main staircase was not yet in place; not a single apartment had been finished. There was no yard and no fence. And, said Abigail, "The great unfinished audience-room [East Room] I make a drying-room of, to hang the clothes in."[2] She also added sarcastically that the president's salary was insufficient to meet the cost of maintaining this enormous pile.

The White House was so poorly protected from the elements when the Adamses moved in that "rain and wind found access even to its best sleeping apartments," recalled Margaret Bayard Smith.[3] A short time later, the ceiling of the so-called audience room collapsed. Not until the administration of President Andrew Jackson was the East Room finally finished in elegant style.

Abigail did like the location of the mansion, however, and in real estate, as is well known, location is everything. Fortunately, the house had not been built in Georgetown, which she said was the "very dirtyest Hole I ever saw." The President's House, as she called it, was beautifully situated in front of the Potomac River with a view of Alexandria. "The country around is romantic," she continued, "but . . . a wilderness at present." So Abigail sighed, accepted her lot, and told her sister that "I am determined to be satisfied and content, to say nothing of inconvenience &c."[4]

Some of the inconvenience, as the early newspapers noted, came from the fact that the yard around the mansion was littered with building materials. This unsightly mess remained for years, and some thought it made the occupant of the house look ridiculous. "I cannot but consider our Presidents as very unfortunate men, if they must live in this dwelling," wrote Secretary of the Treasury Oliver Wolcott. Cold and damp in the winter, it needed a "regiment of servants," he said, to keep it in "tolerable order."[5] And what can you do when workmen's shanties, privies, the remains of bricklaying, the sheds of stonecutters, and muddy holes used for mixing mortar make the house look unsightly and unattractive? Negotiating these hazards in the dark called for special caution lest one "fall into a pit, or stumble over a heap of rubbish." To enter the mansion, a person had to ascend by rough wooden steps a full story above ground. It "is a disgrace to the country," grumbled one man.[6]

Right from the start of construction, many newspapers[7] complained about the house, and especially the cost of completing it. Apparently, the citizens of Washington complained too. The *National Intelligencer,* a Washington newspaper founded in 1800,[8] carried a letter from a reader who was angry over paying county taxes and not getting better roads in the District of Columbia. Instead, he said, the money was appropriated for a "footway from the President's house to George Town, and for an unnecessary Bridge over Rock Creek."[9] Oliver Wolcott agreed. "Immense sums have been squandered in buildings which are but partly finished," he wrote his wife. "No stranger can be here a day and converse with [the citizens] without conceiving himself in the company of crazy people."[10]

Like Abigail Adams, the early newspapers always referred to the chief executive's residence as "the President's House," not "the Presidential Palace," which is what Major Pierre-Charles L'Enfant always called it. The commissioners of the federal district, who had been appointed by President George Washington to survey and purchase land on the eastern side of the Potomac River and provide appropriate buildings for the president, the executive departments and the Congress, also used L'Enfant's term during the early years whenever they advertised in the newspapers for workmen.[11]

The earliest notices to appear in the press about the President's House concerned a call for architectural plans to build the structure, for which premiums were offered as a reward. Because the sale of lots would never bring in the amount of money required to erect all the public buildings needed by the government, it was necessary to negotiate a series of loans, running into the hundreds of thousands of dollars, which the press duly noted. These public buildings, lectured the newspapers, whatever their cost and design, had to be in accord with the "simplicity and purity of our republican government."[12]

In addition, the newspapers quite regularly carried advertisements for workers to complete the President's House. Two dollars a day were offered for "good carpenters and joiners," and a proportional amount for those less skilled. Whenever lots were offered for sale in the District of Columbia, their locations were usually described by the newspapers in relation to their distance from the President's House. So were liquor stores. One such ad identified a grog shop as being "on the Pennsylvania Avenue between the President's House and the Capitol."[13]

The President's House won national press coverage when the cornerstone of the building was laid on October 13, 1792. The nation's newspapers noted that a brass plate was laid on top of a foundation stone located in the southwest corner of the building.[14] A cornerstone was placed on top of the plate, which read:

This first stone of the President's House was laid the 13th day of October, 1792 and in the 17th Year of the Independence of the United States of America.

George Washington, President
Thomas Johnson ⎫
Doctor Steward ⎬ Commissioners
Daniel Carroll ⎭
James Hoban, Architect
Collen Williamson, Master Mason
Vivat Respublica[15]

Eight years later, the press noted the arrival of President Adams in the capital city to reside in the unfinished mansion. "On Saturday last," November 1, 1800, reported the *National Intelligencer*, "the President of the United States arrived in this city, and took up his residence in the house appropriated to him by the commissioners. Though momentarily finished, the part which is completed will afford ample accommodations."[16] But a Washington matron noted the presidential entrance into the city with something of a smirk. "The President with his secretary, Mr. Shaw, passed by in his chariot and four, no retinue, only one servant on horseback."[17]

One of the first official functions in the President's House reported by the newspapers was the Fourth of July celebration of 1801 hosted by the new president, Thomas Jefferson. "About 12 o'clock," said the *National Intelligencer*, "the President was waited upon by the heads of Departments, and other officers civil and military, foreign diplomatic characters, strangers of distinction, the Cherokee chiefs at present on a mission to the seat of government, and most of the respectable citizens of Washington and George Town. Abundant refreshments were served [cakes of various kinds, wine, punch] . . . which may be truly said to have been without alloy," along with a mammoth cheese. The celebration continued until about 2 P.M. As part of the festivities, uniformed companies of militia paraded on the grounds in front of the house, side-stepping a new well that was being dug and other water holes and hazards, "and, after going through a variety of evolutions, saluted the President." Then the United States Marine Band "played a succession of patriotic airs."[18]

The next public occasion at the White House to receive the attention of the press was New Year's Day, January 1, 1802, when a great many people gathered to celebrate "the return of another year, crowned with the continued enjoyment of peace, liberty, and prosperity."[19]

As president, Thomas Jefferson certainly added real style to the house. He began immediately to "fulfil the social duties of the place," said the partisan Republican press, "without alloy," and each day he entertained a company of not more than twelve at dinner.[20] During the congressional session, he hosted groups of government officials; in the off season, distinguished citizens of the District, Georgetown, and Alexandria. He introduced circular shelves and dumbwaiters (these can be seen at Monticello) into the mansion, and he employed a French cook so that his "entertainments," noted Margaret Bayard Smith, combined "republican symplicity" with "Epicurean delicacy." At the touch of a spring on one of his many intriguing gadgets, "little doors flew open, and disclosed within, a goblet of water, a decanter of wine, a plate of light cakes, and a night-taper." Said Jefferson: "I often sit up late, and my wants are thus provided for without keeping a servant up."[21]

Newspaper critics of this new Republican administration did not fail to point out how this servant of the people was living in "a species of regal splendor," in a "great stone house, big enough for two emperors, one pope and the grand lama in the bargain." But Jefferson had a few complaints of his own. When the furniture from the President's House in Philadelphia was finally brought to Washington, it was so worn out that it had to be replaced. But that entailed additional expense, as the newspapers immediately noted. So the House of Representatives resolved itself into a committee of the whole to discuss the matter. Some $15,000 had been allocated in 1800 for furnishing the President's House, $6,000 of which still remained unspent. There was strong opposition to providing additional money beyond the $6,000. From his observation, said Representative Samuel Smith of Maryland, he could "perceive no want of furniture nor elegance" in such parts of the house as were occupied. Nathaniel Macon of North Carolina argued that there was no more reason to furnishing the President's House than those of the heads of departments. If the president cannot live with the sum already provided, he cannot live with any sum, he added. Macon believed that what had already been provided would last for at least fifty years. If we keep increasing the appropriations, he declared, "there would be a great amount of furniture in a few years, by the sums being heaped on each other." Furthermore, "If the style of the furniture was raised so very high, he [Macon] should not be surprised soon if there was to be a proposition to make the salary a little more adequate to the style of the furniture, and raise that too, to bring him up to the style of his furniture." That paragon of virtue, George Washington, unlike this new Republican president, had had no complaints of inadequacy about the furniture purchased during his eight years in office. Moreover, the sums provided were intended solely for the purchase of household goods. But an inventory of what had been purchased recently, said Joseph B. Varnum of Massachusetts, showed an item of seven horses and a carriage, and even a market wagon, together with harnesses. "This plainly evinced that though the House had appropriated $15,000 for household furniture, the president had thought himself authorized to purchase carriages, horses, and perhaps other things which his convenience might suggest." Not only were there improper appropriations, added Samuel Smith, "but the manner in which the money had been laid out" did not comply with the law.

That remark infuriated Federalists. Representative Robert Goodloe Harper of South Carolina angrily complained that Smith's criticism constituted nothing more than a "disposition to trample, very unworthily indeed, upon those who are already fallen," meaning, of course, the former Federalist president, John Adams. Smith responded that he only wished to say that if the money had been laid out for furniture, "the house would have had a better appearance than at present." The House of Representatives then voted down providing any additional funds for furniture.[22]

The President's House, in other words, was a constant drain on the treasury. The press, of course, duly noted congressional squabbling over expenses and the president's life-style. The press, the people of Washington, and a great many congressmen saw the Executive Mansion not as a national symbol, but as a very expensive operation to keep the chief officer of the Republic in "regal splendor."

As might be expected, President Jefferson also demanded numerous architectural changes in the mansion when he took office. He required so many that Benjamin Henry Latrobe was called upon to supervise the alterations. Jefferson sold off the carriage, horses, and harnesses that Adams had bought and asked that the privy built beside the house in 1800 be removed. In its place two water closets were installed upstairs, at either end of the transverse hallway. And the house needed a new roof because the existing one leaked, damaging walls and ruining several pieces of furniture.[23]

Jefferson was also eager to improve the mansion's grounds with trees, shrubs, and flowers indigenous to America, but Congress refused his repeated requests for the necessary funds. However, he did manage to line Pennsylvania Avenue with Lombardy poplars.

Federalist complaints about these "Republican" changes and their cost constantly surfaced in the partisan press during this early national period.[24] Republicans countered by stating that James Madison, the secretary of state, and Albert Gallatin, the secretary of the treasury, could also live in the mansion and pay rent to the president, who would then deposit the money in the treasury. "That is republican and economical," one staunch Jeffersonian brightly declared in response.[25] Apparently, at one point, serious consideration was given to having the department heads live in the President's House and pay rent. Imagine the historic and dramatic, not to mention explosive, scenes that might have ensued if that incredible thought had ever been brought to fruition.

Federalists tended to boycott Jefferson's receptions in the mansion until 1807, when relations with Great Britain took a turn for the worse with the attack upon the USS *Chesapeake* by the British warship *Leopard* on June 22, 1807. The *Chesapeake* was fired upon and boarded, and four seamen were removed. The Republican press carefully noted the presence of Federalists during the Fourth of July celebration that year in the President's House. "On no antecedent occasion has the assemblage been so great; and party spirit, which heretofore had withheld a number of leading federalists from offering any public mark of respect to the chief Magistrate, to the honor of human nature, gave way to the patriotic feelings and unanimity called for by the times." Patriotic airs were played at the reception by the U.S. Marine Band while refreshments were served.[26]

The War of 1812 brought a great influx of people to Washington to conduct business relating to military operations and, for the first time, the District published a guide book listing the names of department officials and clerks, city officers, magistrates, bank directors, and so on. In addition, a picture in *acqua tinta* of the north view of the President's House was put up for sale for the grand sum of fifty cents. As far as is known, the first published view of the house appeared in an engraving for a book by Charles W. Janson, entitled *The Stranger in America*, which appeared in 1807.[27]

The war, of course, brought destruction to Washington when a British army commanded by General Robert Ross and accompanied by Admiral George Cockburn, who had suggested the attack, invaded the District and on August 25, 1814, put it to the torch. The French minister, Louis Barbe Sérurier, who had remained in the city, saw a detachment of soldiers with lighted torches heading for the President's House, and he sent a message to the commanding officer asking that the mansion be spared. "My messenger," Sérurier reported in a dispatch to Talleyrand, the French foreign minister, "found General Ross in the White House, where he was collecting in the drawing room [the present-day Blue Room] all the furniture to be found and preparing to set it on fire." General Ross sent Sérurier assurances that "the king's house," as he called it, would be spared.[28] Of course, it was not.

What is particularly interesting about this dispatch is that Sérurier referred to the mansion as the "White House." Indeed, the same designation was used in a letter signed by "Publius" published in the *Federal Republican* of November 4, 1814. As far as can be determined the first newspaper to refer to the executive mansion as the "White House" was the Baltimore *Whig* on November 22, 1810. Quite possibly residents of the District used the term since the building received its first coat of whitewash in 1798, according to a report of James Hoban.[29]

At least one cabinet officer and several congressmen also used this term. As early as May 19, 1809, Henry Dearborn, secretary of war under President Jefferson, employed it, as did a British official in the spring of 1811. Representative Daniel Webster of New Hampshire wrote a letter on June 10, 1813, to his friend Charles March in which he commented about how badly the war with Great Britain was going for the United States. "There cannot be much sleep in the White-house," he added. Four days later he again spoke about another congressman wishing "to consult the little occupant [James Madison] of the great White House."

During the first half of the nineteenth century, however, newspapers generally referred to the mansion as the "President's House." After 1850 the term "Executive Mansion" became the popular name for the building. It took official action by President Theodore Roosevelt in 1901 before the term "White House" was used exclusively when referring to the executive mansion.[30]

The outrage felt by the American people over the "barbarous conflagration" of their capital city by the British in 1814 was widely reported by the press. "The hate with which *we* have always said *Great Britain* regarded us, is now exhibiting by a Goth-like war," editorialized one newspaper. "How could a nation eminently civilized, conduct itself at Washington with as much barbarity as the old banditti of *Attila,* and *Genseric?* Is not this act of attrocious vengeance *a crime against all humanity?*" European newspapers were extensively quoted in the American press. "THE COSSACKS SPARED PARIS," said the *London Statesman* as reported in *Niles' Weekly Register,* "BUT WE SPARED NOT THE CAPITOL OF AMERICA." "Thus, then, the war is prosecuted in the new world," said a Paris newspaper, "with the same character of fury as for so long a period spread desolation over the old. It there exhibits the same spectacle of devastation and horror."[31]

Washington's *National Intelligencer* reported in an editorial reprinted in all the leading newspapers that Admiral Cockburn was a "mountebank in the city, exhibiting in the streets a gross levity of manner, displaying sundry articles of trifling value of which he had robbed the President's house, and repeating many of the coarse jests and vulgar slang . . . respecting the chief magistrate." The press reported that some $2 million in property was lost during the conflagration and that the justice of the peace, William Thornton, had to appoint a guard at the White House and other buildings to "prevent plunderers who were carrying off articles to the amount of thousands of dollars."[32]

The press also noted that there was talk of moving the seat of government, either temporarily or permanently, and this loose talk elicited their extreme displeasure and anger: "We cannot find language to express our abhorrence and astonishment at the suggestion." It was both unconstitutional and unjust, declared the press. Congress "dare not sanction" such a move. It would be an act of cowardice and defeat.[33]

Suddenly the mood in the country, as reported in the newspapers, had

A View of the President's House in the City of Washington after the Conflagration of the 24th August 1814 reveals only a blackened shell. This was all that remained after the British burned the White House during the War of 1812. This "barbarous conflagration" finally inspired Congress to appropriate sufficient funds for the president to reconstruct the residence. Courtesy of the Library of Congress.

changed about the capital and all its expensive and regal public buildings. Not only did it become a matter of national pride and honor to restore the city, but now the newspapers demanded greater and more beautiful public works. "The public building," said one journal, "instead of being left in that unfinished state, which we have more than once pointed out as a standing reproach to the government; instead of elegant skeletons, half-finished, half-dilapidated structures, we shall, in a few months we hope, be able to boast of the most splendid public edifices in the world — a boast in no way incompatible with the purest principles of Republican government." The burning of the capital was "a blessing in disguise," said the *National Intelligencer*. The "Capitol, President's House, and Executive Offices, will be rebuilt with additional splendor."[34]

Thus at this time, perhaps unconsciously, the press, and probably the American people, started to view the White House and Capitol as national symbols. Said one paper in 1815: "We have the satisfaction of witnessing now a rapid advancement in the repairs, or rather reconstruction, of the Capitol, President's House and Public Offices, under an appropriation made by Congress, and the fostering protection of the national faith."[35]

Somehow the war, the burning of the capital, and the fact that the nation had survived the struggle without dishonor produced a national faith represented by national symbols. Parenthetically, "Uncle Sam" made his first appearance during this so-called forgotten war.

The restored White House received its new occupant, President James Monroe, on Wednesday, September 17, 1817. He stayed only a few days, according to Secretary of State John Quincy Adams, because he was very "apprehensive of the effects of the fresh paint and plastering."[36] But the press was pleased with the splendor of the house. It had been rebuilt "with many improvements in the interior [sic] arrangement of the building; and several rooms are completed for the comfortable accommodation of the President. So that it will no longer be necessary for the chief officer of the government to be chaffering for lodgings." The furniture had not yet arrived; a portion of it had been ordered from France, which caused some indignant citizens to write to the newspapers and object to the White House's being stocked with foreign-made goods.[37]

In this English engraving of 1831 we see the refurbished White House in its
bucolic, park-like setting. The city barely encroaches. Courtesy of the White
House.

There were a number of Louis XVI pieces with brass inlays, carpets, heavy Empire gilt chairs covered in crimson satin and bedecked with gold eagles, a large table for the state dining room set off by a French gilt plateau, French porcelain dinnerware depicting an eagle bearing an olive branch, several Italian mantelpieces with supporting columns in the form of sculptured female figures — ordered without nudity to avoid a public outrage. Foreign visitors commented that the house had been furnished in surprisingly good taste for America.[38]

Since the government provided no White House staff, the cost of maintaining the mansion far exceeded the president's salary of $25,000. The newspapers worried that the amount of money appropriated by Congress was insufficient "to furnish the house on a scale commensurate with its dimensions." Thus the press in just a few years had completely reversed itself. Instead of complaining about the amount of money appropriated to maintain the president in "regal splendor" in the White House, they grumbled about the fact that the appropriation might not be enough.

In President Monroe's message of February 10, 1818, to the Congress about the appropriation — which the newspapers reprinted in toto — he stated that all the furniture procured before 1814 had been destroyed in the fire. "The furniture," he wrote, "is thought to be an object not less deserving attention than the building for which it is intended, both being national objects. . . . For a building so extensive, intended for a purpose exclusively national, in which, in the furniture provided for it, a mingled regard is due to the simplicity and purity of our institutions, and to the character of the people who are represented in it, the sum already appropriated has proved altogether inadequate."

The White House, said Monroe, like the Capitol, was a national institution that represented the American people. It is a "trust," he continued, and as such its care, "in a more especial manner," ought to be taken over by a "public agent" so that it may be guarded and protected for the enjoyment and edification of future generations.[39] The White House, at last, had indeed become a national symbol.

NOTES

I should like to thank Robert Gudmestad, a graduate student at the University of Richmond, for his assistance in the research for this article.

1. Abigail Adams to Mary Cranch, November 21, 1800, *New Letters of Abigail Adams, 1788–1801*, ed. Stewart Mitchell (Boston: Houghton Mifflin Co., 1947), 259–60.

2. Quoted in James Sterling Young, *The Washington Community, 1800–1828* (New York: Columbia University Press, 1966), 45.

3. "President's House Forty Years Ago" [1841], in Margaret Bayard Smith, *The First Forty Years of Washington Society* (New York: Charles Scribner's Sons, 1906), 384.

4. Adams to Cranch, November 21, 1800, *New Letters*, 257.

5. Oliver Wolcott to Mrs. Wolcott, July 4, 1800, in George Gibbs, *Memoirs of the Administrations of Washington and John Adams*, 2 vols. (New York: W. Van Norcer, 1846), 2:377.

6. Charles William Janson, *The Stanger in America* (London: Albion Press, 1807), 213; Mrs. Thornton's diary quoted in Wilhelmus Bogart Bryan, *A History of the National Capital*, 2 vols. (New York: Macmillan Co., 1914), 1:377 n. 3.

7. At the start of the nineteenth century, the *National Intelligencer* and its weekly version, the *Universal Gazette*, began publication. The *Washington Gazette* and the *Centinel of Liberty* or *George-town and Washington Advertiser* appeared in Georgetown. There was also the *Alexandria Advertiser*. See Constance McLaughlin Green, *Washington: Capital City, 1789–1950* (Princeton: Princeton University Press, 1962), 18–19, 36. Despite the newspaper criticism of the mansion after the Adamses moved in, the *Boston Gazette* on February 5, 1798, thought the house rather grand. "The president's House in Washington," wrote the editor, "built of white free stone, is in length 175 feet 7 inches, and breadth 83 feet 5 inches — rooms 26½ feet long — 19 feet high — walls outside, 2 feet 9 inches, and inside 2 feet. The beautiful imagery appears pleasing to the face, and captivating to the eye, there were two stories of this delightful edifice, compleated in May 1796, and since the guarantee of the new loan, they go on rapid in building." Quoted in John W. Reps, *Washington on View: The Nation's Capital Since 1790* (Chapel Hill: University of North Carolina Press, 1991), 40.

8. The *Intelligencer* was started and operated by Samuel Harrison Smith, who sold it in 1810. Smith's wife was Margaret Bayard Smith.

9. December 3, 1800. The writer signed himself "Justice."

10. Wolcott to Mrs. Wolcott, July 4, 1800, in Gibbs, *Memoirs*, 2:378.

11. Bryan, *History of the National Capital*, 1:120, 149–50.

12. *National Intelligencer*, March 11, 1801.

13. *Centinel of Liberty*, November 7, 1800.

14. Despite several recent attempts with high-tech equipment, this cornerstone has not been found. It is believed that the equipment will have to be more advanced before the stone can be found.

15. Charleston, S.C., *City Gazette & Daily Advertiser*, November 15, 1792.

16. *National Intelligencer*, November 3, 1800. See also *Centinel of Liberty*, November 4, 1800.

17. Quoted in Bryan, *History of the National Capital*, 1:376 n. 1.

18. *National Intelligencer*, July 6, 7, October 24, 1801. Margaret B. Smith to Mary Ann Smith, July 5, 1801, in Smith, *Forty Years*, 30.

19. *National Intelligencer*, January 2, 1805.

20. See accounts of several celebrations in the *National Intelligencer*, July 6, 1803 and 1804; January 2, July 8, 1805. According to the March 20, 1801, *Intelligencer*, Jefferson moved into the house on March 19, 1801.

21. Smith, *Forty Years*, 390, 391–93.

22. *Washington Advertiser*, March 11, 1801.

23. *National Intelligencer*, October 24, 1803.

24. It would be a mistake to give the impression that the President's House was mentioned frequently in the press during the early national period. Aside from the New Year's Day and Fourth of July receptions, and the squabbling in Congress over costs, the press rarely talked about the house. It was not the center for national news that it is today.

25. *Alexandria Advertiser*, May 25, 1801, quoted in Bryan, *History of the National Capital*, 1:405, 419.

26. *National Intelligencer*, July 8, 1807.

27. Ibid., June 1, 1813; Bryan, *History of the National Capital*, 1:618n.

28. Bryan, *History of the National Capital*, 1:627.

29. Ibid., 313 nn. 3, 4; statement "Origin of the Name 'White House' " issued by the Office of the Curator, 1984.

30. Webster to March, June 10, 14, 1813, in *The Papers of Daniel Webster, Correspondence*, ed. Charles Wiltse (Hanover: Dartmouth College/University Press of New England, 1974), 1:148, 150; "Origin of the Name 'White House.' "

31. *Niles' Weekly Register*, September 10, December 31, 1814.

32. *National Intelligencer*, August 31, September 7, 1814; *Niles' Weekly Register*, September 10, 1814.

33. *National Intelligencer*, September 2, 1814.

34. Ibid., March 30, 1815.

35. Ibid., August 3, 1815. For 1817 the Congress appropriated $109,180.78 for the rebuilding of the President's House.

36. John Quincy Adams, *Memoirs of John Quincy Adams*, ed. Charles Francis Adams, 12 vols. (Philadelphia: J. B. Lippincott, 1874–1877), 4:7.

37. *National Intelligencer*, December 29, 1817.

38. Harry Ammon, *James Monroe: The Quest for National Identity* (New York: McGraw-Hill, 1971), 400–401, 403. It should be noted that for the first few years Monroe used his own furniture.

39. *National Intelligencer*, February 11, 1818.

Chapter

America's House:

The Bully Pulpit
on Pennsylvania Avenue

Richard Norton Smith

In the bleak, intemperate spring of 1932, the president of the United States found three children on his doorstep. Their father was an unemployed laborer from Detroit, arrested on a charge of auto theft while en route home from a job-hunting trip out West. Soon after, the trio of unhappy youngsters set off for the nation's capital. Believing that the man in the White House was possessed of unlimited powers, they were determined to lay their case before him.

The president's advisers thought him far too busy to hear such an appeal. There was, after all, a worldwide depression to combat, a sullen and jittery nation to reassure, a political campaign to organize. Herbert Hoover thought otherwise. As he put it, "Three children resourceful enough to manage to get to Washington to see me are going to see me."

"Now, Bernice," Hoover remarked to their thirteen-year-old leader, "tell me the whole story." As he listened, the muscles in his face twitched in an effort to control his emotions, and when she was finished, the president said that there must be a great deal of good in any man whose children were so devoted. Then he took from his desk a keepsake for each. "I want you to have this to remember me by," he said. "Now run along and go straight home. Dad will be waiting for you."

A few minutes later, presidential press secretary Theodore Joslin en-

31

tered the Oval Office to find his employer staring out the window, fighting back tears. "Get that father out of jail immediately," Hoover commanded. Joslin asked permission to share the highly charged encounter
with the press. It was exactly the kind of story that would humanize the
dour chief executive, drawing out the compassion that had once made
him a global hero. Hoover would have none of it. The children might
remember his act of kindness. But neither it, nor they, would be ex-
ploited for political advantage.[1] The Quaker president, uncomfortable
with displays of emotion, elevated his shortcomings to the level of prin-
ciple. "This is not a showman's job," he said on another occasion. "You
can't make a Teddy Roosevelt out of me."[2]

Ironically, Hoover had more in common with TR than he acknowledged. His path-breaking White House Conference on Child Health and
Welfare was a direct descendant of Roosevelt's 1909 White House Conference on Children. So were more than thirty White House commissions, blue ribbon panels, and study groups designed to curb Prohibition-era lawlessness, attack illiteracy, promote home ownership,
coordinate relief for the jobless, and project social trends for Washington
policymakers as severely rational as Hoover himself.[3]

But there was a crucial difference. Whereas TR personalized the role
of presidential advocate, putting himself always at the center of events,
Hoover tried instead to institutionalize his Quaker compassion. His un-
inspiring speeches moved critics to say that while Lincoln split rails,
Hoover split infinitives. Even sympathetic observers blamed the president for failing the supreme test of leadership articulated by the first
Roosevelt — that of marshaling public opinion by dramatizing himself
and his program. Franklin Roosevelt knew better. "The presidency is
not merely an administrative office," he said. "That is the least of it. It
is preeminently a place of moral leadership."[4]

Whatever else divided them, both Hoover and Roosevelt governed in
the long shadow of Theodore Rex, whose bully pulpit reflected his celebrated theory of presidential stewardship. According to TR, a modern
president was "bound actively and affirmatively to do all he could for
the people. . . . I did not usurp power," he added, not altogether convinc-
ingly, "but I did greatly broaden the use of executive power."[5]

Under TR the White House became a crowded theater peopled by melodramatic heroes and villains. On stage was a never-ending morality play scripted, directed, and performed by the president himself. Roosevelt summoned coal magnates and striking workers to settle their differences under his watchful gaze. He derided "malefactors of wealth," much as his cousin thirty years later would strike out at the "economic royalists" in whose hatred he gloried. As the first of this century's presidential swashbucklers, Theodore Roosevelt rarely shied away from the personal pronoun — indeed, when running off the president's first message to Congress, the Government Printing Office was said to have run out of capital *I*'s. The president had opinions on everything and took a child's delight in stating them, from the virtues of phonetic spelling and the glories of the great outdoors to the pernicious theories of "race suicide" held by advocates of birth control to the dangers of "embalmed beef." He denounced George Bernard Shaw as a "blue rumped ape" and pacifists as "flubdubs and mollycoddles."[6]

Roosevelt remade the physical White House as he redefined its symbolic place at the heart of the nation's political life. "Smash the glass houses," he thundered, with the same glee he reserved for his enemies in Congress, and down came the sprawling conservatories familiar since Buchanan's time. Out went President Arthur's Tiffany screens and President McKinley's potted palms. Moose heads took up residence in the State Dining Room. Roosevelt himself moved his office into a new West Wing built to his specifications, where reporters for the first time had their own quarters from which to keep tabs on the president and his no-less-colorful family.[7]

When the restoration was finished, 1600 Pennsylvania Avenue harkened back to the austere traditions of the early Republic. White House coachmen donned livery and cockades recalling the stiff formality of the Federalist era. This was only appropriate, for while TR is credited with inventing the "bully pulpit," he was in truth carrying on a custom as old as the nation's highest office. Long before there was a United States, there was a powerful sense of American exceptionalism. Even before there was a presidency, there was Alexander Hamilton's assertion in the *Federalist Papers* that an energetic and unified executive posed no threat to America's newly won liberties. Indeed, judged Hamilton, "Energy in the executive is a leading character in the definition of good government," essential to the common defense, the administration of laws, and the protection of property and individual freedom against the assaults of faction, ambition, and anarchy.[8]

In his first inaugural, George Washington struck an almost Roose-veltian tone. "There is no truth more thoroughly established," he said, "than that there exists an indissoluble union between virtue and happiness; between duty and advantage."[9] The United States, Washington implied, could only flourish as a Republic of Virtue, her president setting an example and, on occasion, using his exalted position to teach, admonish, and publicize. What else but moral suasion went into Washington's Farewell Address, Jefferson's embargo, Monroe's doctrine of nonintervention by Europe in the affairs of the New World, Jackson's scathing veto of the Bank of the United States, or Lincoln's Emancipation Proclamation?

Moreover, long before TR donned his ministerial robes, the American congregation was accustomed to projecting its values and aspirations upon the man in the pulpit. Equating morality with democratic principles, newly independent Americans frowned on conduct reminiscent of the Old World's numbing protocol. Thus plain-living lawmakers, ever alert to signs of aristocratic pretense, criticized President Washington for his weekly levees, his formal dinners — even the bow he substituted for handshaking. In 1801 Thomas Jefferson became the first president to shake hands and the last to greet foreign envoys in his dressing gown and slippers. However elaborate his dinners, however fine his wines, Jefferson and his successors took pains to identify the President's House with the people who paradoxically loved both its grandeur and its openness.

Amid the shifting currents of Jacksonian America, the White House became a pulpit in the plain church of frontier democracy. And woe to those who defiled the tabernacle. John Quincy Adams was denounced for his purchase of a billiard table with the people's money. Yet his real crime was a bold program of internal improvements, topped off by a national observatory Adams memorably labeled "a lighthouse of the sky."[10] This sounded not only wasteful, but suspiciously at odds with republican simplicity. Never mind that Adams's successor, Andrew Jackson, spent over $45,000 on elegant furnishings, importing china and crystal from France and rebuilding the East Room to give it what one aide called "an air of thundering grandeur," complete with triumphal arch, to welcome the Hero of New Orleans.[11]

Jackson may have lacked the special aura that revolutionary service imparted to each of his predecessors, but he understood instinctively how a president willing to use the symbolic tools at his command — not excluding the White House itself — could rally the nation behind his programs and against enemies, real or imagined. The mob scene that inaugurated the Jackson era is engraved in American mythology. Less familiar is the climax of those stormy years. Early in 1835, admiring New Yorkers presented Jackson with a fourteen-hundred-pound cheese, an object lustily cheered by crowds along a three-hundred-mile route. For two years the gift sat in the White House vestibule, a pungent symbol of the president's solidarity with the common man. Then, on Washington's Birthday, 1837, Jackson invited the entire city — mechanics as well as congressmen — to be his guests in devouring the cheese. According to a local journalist, "Mr. Van Buren was there to eat cheese; Mr. Webster was there to eat cheese. . . . All you heard was cheese; all you smelled was cheese."[12]

The aroma of New York cheddar was still in the air when Mr. Van Buren was confronted with America's first great depression. Lacking Jackson's genius for confrontation, the dapper Van Buren was further hampered by opposition Whigs who had learned their lessons from a master of public incitement. A Pennsylvania congressman named Charles Ogle published a savage burlesque entitled "The Royal Splendor of the President's Palace." What would hard-working Americans think, Ogle demanded, of their popularly chosen leader ensconced in a "Palace as splendid as that of the Caesars. . . . What, sir, will the honest locofoco say to Mr. Van Buren for spending the People's cash on FOREIGN FANNY KEMBLE GREEN FINGER CUPS, in which to wash his pretty, tapering, soft, white lilly-fingers, after dining on fricandeau de veau and omelette souffle?"[13]

The White House was less pulpit than punching bag in the years leading up to Fort Sumter. So unpopular was John Tyler, the self-styled President Without a Party, that Congress withheld appropriations for upkeep and refurbishment. Both were restored in 1845 when the Polks moved in, even as fashionable Washingtonians made sport of Sarah Polk's strictures against Sabbath dancing and card parties. According to Sam Houston, the only problem with President Polk was that he drank too much water.[14] Houston notwithstanding, Polk's successors filled the White House with Victorian morality.

Rutherford and Lucy Hayes, for example, enjoyed nightly hymn singing. Neither was reluctant to make the White House a personal platform from which to extol the virtues of temperance. While history has credited the policy to "Lemonade Lucy," the dry spell that coincided with the Hayes presidency was largely the president's own doing. Said Hayes, "It seemed to me that the example of excluding liquors from the White House would be wise and useful, and would be approved by good people generally."[15] Left unaddressed was whether good people would thereby be more likely to vote Republican.

Cosmopolitan Chester Arthur enjoyed a revenge of sorts when he cleaned out the old house before Louis Tiffany's redecoration in the 1880s. Among the items Arthur disposed of was a sideboard given to Lucy Hayes by the Women's Christian Temperance Union. A Washington saloon keeper bought it and kept it, filled with liquors, in his bar on Pennsylvania Avenue.[16]

These were isolated gestures of moral uplift, all but lost in an era of party government that was anything but saintly and a Congress that was anything but subservient. Yet forces were gathering that would redress the imbalance between the executive and legislative branches. By the end of the century, America was a world power, however reluctant. Inevitably, foreign policy, and especially the conduct of war, concentrated authority in the presidential office. Thanks to Hearst and other press lords, newspaper readership quadrupled, creating fresh opportunities for any leader willing to thrust himself and his ideas center stage.

Enter Theodore Roosevelt, if not the most effective of presidents, then certainly the most outspoken. Said humorist Irvin Cobb, "You had to hate the Colonel a whole lot to keep from loving him."[17] Cartoonists loved him most of all. They depicted TR as Old Dutch Cleanser, scouring the grimy corridors of American politics. Thenceforth it was not enough for an American president to meet his dual obligations as head of state and head of government. Beginning with Roosevelt, he also had

An engraving depicting President Andrew Jackson's 1829 inaugural festivities at the White House. The crowd's pressure forced him to flee out a window to a hotel. Courtesy of the White House.

to serve as a national conscience of sorts, an adviser at large on things in general. The White House became more than a shrine to American democracy; it was a temple of the cult of presidential personality that caused Walter Lippmann to define the first Roosevelt as "a working model for a possible American statesman at the beginning of the 20th century."[18]

With the perspective of time, we can look beyond the histrionics to probe TR's actual achievements. On the question of trusts, for example, he trusted rather more than he busted, leaving it to his prosaic successor, William Howard Taft, to file more — and more important — suits against industrial combinations. Even so, Roosevelt placed his stamp upon the office and the age. "While president," he said afterward, "I have *been* president, emphatically."[19] Domination was not achieved without cost. Living at a higher pitch than other men, TR naturally risked wearing out his welcome, a still greater occupational hazard for later chief executives governing under the harsh glare of the television spotlight.

As Emerson said, every hero is at last a bore. And yet, for all TR's exhibitionism, there was something inspiring about his campaign for economic democracy, waged on a level with Andrew Jackson's crusade for political democracy in the 1830s. It gave substance to his legend and resonance to his ex cathedra pronouncements. And it forever redefined the presidency as the sole voice authentically representing *all* the American people.

The bully pulpit reached new heights of influence under Woodrow Wilson, a lifelong student of parliamentary debate and a brilliant lay preacher in an oratory-loving age. Recognizing that only public opinion was sufficient to compel Congress to follow a president's lead, Wilson skillfully employed what he called "the glare of pitiless publicity" to secure passage of his New Freedom legislation. He became the first chief executive since John Adams to take his case directly to Capitol Hill. "That's the sort of thing Roosevelt would have loved to do," said the first Mrs. Wilson after one such appearance. "Yes," her husband replied with a Cheshire cat smile, "I think I have put one over on Teddy."[20]

As Wilson reaped the harvest of Rooseveltian reforms, the White House became a magnet for true believers of every stripe. Eighty years

President Theodore Roosevelt comfortably ensconced in his White House office. Courtesy of the Sean C. Kettelkamp Collection.

before Haitian Americans protesting U.S. immigration policies gathered outside the president's door, or Right-to-Lifers prayed in the middle of Pennsylvania Avenue, Wilson's 1913 inauguration was enlivened by the presence of hundreds of suffragists tramping the streets of Washington with banners that read, "Tell Your Troubles to Woodrow." On another occasion, female protesters, angered over the president's failure to apply his belief in self-determination to the voteless women of America, chained themselves to the White House fence.[21]

Wilson's stirring wartime appeals combined with White House image making to make him the symbol of America's fighting men. Millions of Americans saw their war president in newsreels. "We Take Our Hats Off to You, Mr. Wilson" became a popular tune in this most musically prolific of conflicts. The selling of the president gained new momentum after the White House led the nation in observing meatless Mondays and wheatless Wednesdays as ordained by Herbert Hoover's Food Administration. One gasless Sunday, Wilson and his second wife were driven to church in a horse and carriage. Soon a flock of well-publicized sheep appeared on the White House lawn, their wool auctioned off to benefit the Red Cross. The First Lady, whose immoderate pride in her Native American ancestry had earned her the not-altogether-flattering nickname of Pocahontas, was redubbed Little Bo Peep. Unfortunately, the economy drive cost more than it saved when the sheep began devouring White House shrubbery and flowers.[22]

Through it all, Wilson evangelized before a global audience with messianic fervor. His phrases glittered: peace without victory, open covenants openly arrived at, a war to end all wars. Yet by raising hopes so high, the apostle of self-determination sowed the seeds of his own downfall. By casting 1918 and 1920 as "solemn referendums," Wilson repeated Teddy Roosevelt's mistake of equating presidential righteousness with American self-interest. His eloquence did not fail him, but his judgment did, and, in a tragic coda, he lived out the last eighteen months of his presidency a broken figure. Outside the White House, gossiping tourists pointed to a set of iron bars put over the windows in the nineteenth century, and whispered they were really intended to keep a mentally deranged Wilson from escaping his captors.

Twelve years later, Franklin Roosevelt brought his own formidable

powers of persuasion to the presidency. "I want to be a preaching president like my cousin," he said before inscribing John Adams's famous
prayer over the fireplace of the State Dining Room.[23] A depression-weary
public responded overwhelmingly to the new messenger and his message of hope. Roosevelt's inaugural address drew 460,000 letters. One
clerk handled all of Herbert Hoover's White House mail; FDR needed
fifty to keep abreast of the tide. Reporters were similarly grateful for the
first truly unstructured presidential press conferences, more than three
hundred of which were held in FDR's first term alone.[24]

By the mid-1930s, millions of Americans could listen to a president
in their own homes. Aiding his honey-on-toast baritone was a keen
sense of timing and an instinctive grasp of the dangers of overexposure.
In twelve years FDR conducted just thirty of his celebrated "fireside
chats," and even then he shied away from direct partisan appeals, preferring to use the radio platform to ingratiate himself with listeners
around the kitchen tables of America. So he spoke of "priming the
pump" to explain his deficit spending policies and of loaning Churchill's Britain a garden hose to put out the fire started by Hitler and his
Nazi arsonists.

Supremely confident, Roosevelt even had some advice for adversaries.
"Wendell Willkie talks too much," he told intimates early in 1944.
"You have to know how to strike a chord." The president lifted his
hands high in the air before bringing them down again as if performing
on a piano at Carnegie Hall. "Then you wait," he continued. "Then you
strike the chord again."[25]

The war years saw a fresh surge of moral energy, cresting in the high-
minded, if controversial, sermonizing of the First Lady. Eleanor Roosevelt was not the first presidential wife to address the nation via radio.
Lou Henry Hoover had appealed for assistance to victims of the Great
Depression and unwittingly touched off a national uproar in the summer of 1929 by inviting the wife of a black congressman from Chicago
to take tea at the White House. Many in the South were outraged at
what they deemed a calculated offense to the region's racial sensibili-
ties. The Texas legislature went so far as to urge the president's impeachment. Mrs. Hoover apologized to her husband. "Never mind,

Lou," he told her. "One of the advantages of orthodox religion is that it provides a hot hell for the Texas legislature."[26]

Then came Eleanor. Two days after her husband's first inauguration, she stood in the Red Room clutching a box of candied fruit as an offering to thirty-five newspaperwomen summoned for the first press conference ever conducted by a First Lady. Thereafter, Mondays at 11:30 A.M. were enlivened by the latest sampling of Mrs. Roosevelt's views. She denounced sweatshops and child labor, urged more money for teachers' salaries, and described the seven-and-a-half-cent lunch she served once a week to her long-suffering husband. According to journalist Bess Furman, "At the President's press conferences, all the world's a stage; at Mrs. Roosevelt's, all the world's a school."[27]

The Roosevelt White House reflected its occupants' sympathy for the underdog. Mrs. Roosevelt welcomed black sharecroppers and threw an annual garden party for every Washington woman in federal clerical work. In November 1939, the First Lady invited the officers of the American Youth Congress to a White House lunch following their appearance before the House Committee on Un-American Activities. She convened an East Room gathering on "the cause and cure of war" chaired by feminist pioneer Carrie Chapman Catt. When war closed the mansion to visitors, the president's wife conducted tours for wounded GIs. She became still more visible — and controversial — through her daily newspaper column, "My Day," her radio speeches, and her lecture tours. Said Adolf Hitler, "Eleanor Roosevelt is America's real ruler."[28]

Be that as it may, after 1933, the bully pulpit had to be enlarged to accommodate the First Lady as well as her husband. Indeed, any First Lady without a compelling cause was viewed as sadly deficient in public responsibility. Lady Bird Johnson supported Head Start and beautification. Half a century after Lou Hoover lifted the ban on pregnant women at White House receptions, Betty Ford promoted the Equal Rights Amendment; Nancy Reagan convened an antidrug summit featuring the wives of eight other world leaders. And, of course, Barbara Bush spurred literacy programs from coast to coast.

By mid-century, the Oval Office was the most famous room in America. Everyone, it seemed, agreed with Harry Truman that persuasion was the chief business of the modern presidency. Thanks to the coaxial cable, presidents exhorted us as never before. Truman was first to address the nation on television. Dwight Eisenhower permitted his press conferences to be filmed, a practice JFK refined, to dazzle the most cynical of reporters.

During these years there was no shortage of memorable appeals — from the Truman Doctrine and Ike's Atoms for Peace to JFK's trumpet calls to national sacrifice, Richard Nixon's Silent Majority, and George Bush's insistence that Iraqi aggression in Kuwait would not stand. Yet over time unlimited access to the public airwaves tended to diminish the impact of presidential evangelism. If familiarity did not breed contempt, it most certainly bred skepticism. This should come as no surprise. Next to members of our family and close friends, Americans probably spend more time with our presidents than with anyone else. At the very least, we invite them into our living rooms nightly. Consider: how many television characters are still welcome after eight seasons on the air? Why should presidents be exempt from our mass infatuation with the new — from New Deals and New Frontiers to New Beginnings and more New Nixons than anyone can count?

In any event, the spontaneity of TR's day is long past, submerged in a rising tide of media advisers, inflated rhetoric, Rose Garden ceremonies, and cool blue backdrops. Returning to the White House one day to find the latest in an unending series of photo ops, President Kennedy could barely conceal his anger. "Not more beauty queens," he blurted out. "Eisenhower was right!"[29] He had a point. For at a time when image was increasingly confused with substance, Dwight Eisenhower alone seemed willing to forgo stage effects to practice what Fred Greenstein has called "hidden hand leadership." To one aide Ike explained, "The job is to convince, not to publicize." But few were inclined to follow his example.[30]

From leading public opinion it was but a short, inevitable step toward manipulating it. As the White House became enmeshed in what has been called the permanent campaign, pollsters and focus groups guided modern presidents in tailoring their words. Public relations gestures proliferated. Lyndon Johnson turned the lights out in a famous economy drive. Gerald Ford proposed to Whip Inflation Now. Invitations to Jimmy Carter's inauguration were printed on recycled paper; the president-elect walked down Pennsylvania Avenue in the inaugural parade and wore a cardigan sweater in the Oval Office as evidence of his Everyman appeal. Ronald Reagan renamed an unpopular MX missile the Peacekeeper. At evening press conferences, Reagan moved his East Room podium to emphasize a more stately backdrop.

Starting with TR's Square Deal, activist presidents have demanded a verbal signature — until Richard Nixon tried in vain to rouse public enthusiasm for his New American Revolution. Following the disastrous 1969 White House Conference on Nutrition and Health, at which the president received less applause than the Reverend Ralph Abernathy, planners were careful to place the 1970 White House Conference on Children in the hands of Nixon loyalists.[31] Nixon's later decision to bomb Haiphong Harbor prompted the Committee to Re-Elect the President to spend over $8,000 on newspaper advertisements and telegrams to the White House supporting the action.[32]

None of this is exactly new. Napoleon set up a press office that he called the Bureau of Public Opinion; its function was "to manufacture political trends to order." By the mid-1980s, the Great Communicator, Ronald Reagan, could rely upon three people in the Office of Communication, ten more in the Office of Speech Writing and Research, two in the Office of Media Relations and Planning, fourteen in the Office of Public Liaison, three in the Office of Public Affairs, two in the Office of Communication Planning, fourteen in the Office of the Press Secretary, and five in the Office of News Summary and Audio Service.[33]

Ironically, the modern president's greatest danger lies in the very activism first displayed by Theodore Roosevelt. At the start of a two-week period in June 1979, a time when President Jimmy Carter was working around the clock to convince Congress to approve the Panama Canal Treaty, the president made the evening news with an offhand comment that he would "whip Senator Kennedy's ass" if the latter ran against him in 1980. Two days after this, Carter introduced proposals for national health insurance. Then he left for Vienna to sign the SALT II Agreements. Then he returned to address Congress and the nation on U.S.–Soviet relations. The next day he was again on the news presiding over a ceremony featuring the installation of solar panels at the White House. There he urged Americans to support this and other alternatives to fossil fuels. Three days after that, he left for a World Economic Conference.[34]

A dozen years later, our lives are dominated by television, a medium which fractures time, annihilates distance, and warps perspective. It leads us to believe that problems can be solved in sixty minutes, just as Jessica Fletcher each week resolves a murder before the last fade-out and a final plug for Miracle-Gro and the Chrysler LeBaron. Television has become the Big Brother of modern life, a shadow government and a parody of democracy in action. Candidates play to it; presidents govern by it. In scheduling his 1978 State of the Union Address, Carter had to avoid preempting such popular shows as "Three's Company" and "Laverne and Shirley."

Television homogenizes society. It puts labels on people who should be seen as individuals. And then it pits those labels against each other in dramatic, if often trivial, confrontations. President versus Congress. Dan Quayle versus Murphy Brown. Arsenio Hall versus Jay Leno. Us versus Them.

All this came back to me with renewed force when Hurricane Andrew devastated much of southern Florida in 1992. President Bush, in the best bully pulpit tradition, took to the airwaves to appeal for voluntary assistance and donations to the Red Cross. No sooner did his five-minute address end than CNN, the nation's network of record, immediately switched to Homestead Air Force Base to seek the reaction of four victims of the storm who had lost their homes. Not surprisingly, their enthusiasm for the president's action was muted.

All of which leads to a final haunting paradox. As the network domination of old gives way, and the fragmentation of the nation's media finds reflection in a less cohesive, less informed society, it becomes harder than ever for presidents to command attention on their terms. At the very least, the preacher in the pulpit is in danger of being drowned out by the electronic choir.

More recently, there has been speculation about a post-modernist presidency — even a so-called pointillist presidency — sustained by attention to a thousand local issues, often at the expense of overarching national themes. Certainly, the media tools are in place — the satellite dishes and restless affiliates, the cable outlets and shortened attention spans of the MTV generation. Such a development would be tragic, I think, if only because there are so few unifying institutions in modern America, so few symbols as enduring or potentially constructive as the White House.

For a president to touch people's hearts, he must look beyond their pocketbooks, beyond his own standing in the polls, beyond transient issues and manufactured controversies, to the promises we Americans made to one another in the charters of our nationhood. Promises long delayed. Promises of inclusion. Promises of political, social, and economic justice. Promises recalled in very different ways by Andrew Jackson, Theodore Roosevelt, Woodrow Wilson, Franklin Roosevelt, and Lyndon Johnson, among others.

In an age of widespread cynicism, one might logically predict that the bully pulpit will be employed to maximum advantage only when

1. It addresses a topic of transcendent moral significance;

2. It engages an audience receptive to an appeal that goes beyond short-term self-interest;

3. It enlists the energies and eloquence of a president who is willing to court defeat for a cause he believes in.

The cold war was such a defining issue. Race still is. And here the twentieth-century White House is studded with examples of bold leadership — TR's dinner invitation to Booker T. Washington; Eleanor Roosevelt's resignation from the Daughters of the American Revolution; Dwight Eisenhower's showdown in Little Rock; and LBJ's searing promise to enact a Voting Rights Act "because justice and morality demand it." At such times the bully pulpit becomes synonymous with the house that reflects so much of America's history and so many of our hopes.

In the spring of 1965, soon after Bloody Sunday at the Edmund Pettus Bridge in Selma, President Johnson invited Alabama governor George Wallace to the White House for a dose of Johnsonian persuasion. Afterward a shaken Wallace remarked that had he stayed in the Oval Office any longer, "he'd have had *me* coming out for civil rights!"[35] That summer, before Vietnam and Watergate eroded the moral authority of his office, President Johnson opened the White House to the leading lights of American art, music, and literature. Poet Robert Lowell boycotted the festival to show his opposition to administration policies in Southeast Asia.

But hundreds of other artists came. At the end of a long day of paintings, sculpture, ballet, films, and poetry readings, a White House staff member found the great jazz singer Sarah Vaughan sobbing in her dressing room.

"What's the matter?" she asked Miss Vaughan.

"Nothing is the matter. It's just that twenty years ago when I came to Washington I couldn't even get a hotel room, and tonight I sang for the President of the United States in the White House — and then, he asked me to dance with him. It is more than I can stand!"[36]

On such occasions, sublime in their symbolism, it is again possible to renew the old faith in a presidency that doesn't merely administer our government but that embodies our ideals of inclusive democracy. A presidency that combines TR's zeal and Wilson's eloquence with FDR's shrewdness, LBJ's passion, Ronald Reagan's persuasiveness, and, yes, Herbert Hoover's Quaker rationalism. And which does so with the unique moral authority conferred by a house that for two hundred years has served this country as totem and target.

NOTES

1. Theodore Joslin, *Hoover off the Record* (Garden City, N.Y.: Doubleday, Doran, 1934), 9–11. Joslin also revealed a radio appeal planned at the behest of Mrs. Charles Lindbergh following the 1932 kidnapping of her infant son. Hoover's speech was canceled at the last minute when the boy's father told the White House to expect "an important development." That same night, police discovered the child's remains near the Lindbergh home.

2. Richard Norton Smith, *An Uncommon Man: The Triumph of Herbert Hoover* (New York: Simon & Schuster, 1984), 33. Hoover had no intention of emulating TR's headline-grabbing cousin, either, rejecting out of hand a suggestion, in the wake of Governor Roosevelt's electrifying flight to Chicago to accept his party's 1932 nomination, that *he* go aloft accompanied by Charles Lindbergh and former president Calvin Coolidge.

3. Among TR's numerous blue ribbon panels were the Committees on Public Lands, Inland Waterways, National Conservation, and Country Life. Their members, volunteers all, presented a sharp contrast, the president asserted, to "the traditional clerical apathy which has so often been the distinguishing note

of government work in Washington." Theodore Roosevelt, *Autobiography* (New York: Macmillan Co., 1917), 399.

Prior to the 1930 White House Conference on Child Health and Welfare, the organizationally minded Hoover had one hundred committees of twelve members each doing preparatory spadework for a full year. Less successful was Hoover's Wickersham Commission, chaired by William Howard Taft's attorney general and charged with investigating Prohibition-era lawlessness. The committee's contradictory findings earned it the derisive name of Liquor-sham.

4. Thomas A. Bailey, *Presidential Greatness* (New York: Appleton-Century-Crofts, 1966), 209.

5. Roosevelt, *Autobiography*, 389. For an exposition of TR's celebrated Lincoln-Buchanan theory of presidential leadership, see 395–98.

6. Bailey, *Presidential Greatness*, 200–201. British writer John Morley concluded that America's energetic young executive was a mix of Saint Paul and Saint Vitus. Following the shocking exposé of conditions in the meat-packing industry, Roosevelt appointed yet another government commission to investigate the problem and focus public outrage toward Capitol Hill, where pending legislation to assure purer food and safer drugs needed all the popular pressure that TR and Upton Sinclair together could generate. Opined the *New York Evening Post:*

> Mary had a little lamb
> And when she saw it sicken
> She shipped it off to Packingtown
> And now it's labeled chicken.

Joseph Gardner, *Departing Glory: Theodore Roosevelt as Ex-President* (New York: Charles Scribner's Sons, 1973), 80.

7. The White House Historical Association, *The White House: An Historical Guide* (Washington: White House Historical Association, 1991), 140. In truth, TR's 1902 renovation was part of a larger "back to L'Enfant" movement aimed at restoring the nation's capital to the original vision of the French urban planner (and urged by the McMillan Commission in 1901). The irrepressible Alice Roosevelt cared nothing for commissions; she was merely pleased to be rid of White House furnishings reminiscent of "late General Grant and early Pullman." Bess Furman, *White House Profile* (Indianapolis: Bobbs-Merrill, 1951), 268. Pugnacious to the last, TR chiseled off Charles McKim's elegant State Dining Room mantel containing lions' heads and, early in 1909, replaced it with one featuring the American bison. For further details of the 1902 reconstruction, see Charles Hurd, *The White House: A Biography* (New York: Harper and Brothers, 1940), 226–44.

8. Clinton Rossiter, ed., *The Federalist Papers* (New York: New American Library, 1961), 423.

9. W. B. Allen, ed., *George Washington: A Collection* (Indianapolis: Liberty Fund, 1988), 462.

10. Jack Shepherd, *Cannibals of the Heart* (New York: McGraw-Hill, 1980), 303. It did Adams's cause no good when a pro-administration journalist in Philadelphia rushed to defend the billiard table on the grounds that such an object was de rigeur in "the houses of the rich and great in Europe." For Adams's sweeping asserting of federal authority — astronomical observatories and all — see Samuel Flagg Bemis, *John Quincy Adams and the Union* (New York: Alfred A. Knopf, 1956), 60–70.

11. Robert V. Remini, *Andrew Jackson and the Course of American Democracy, 1833–45* (New York: Harper & Row, 1984), 389.

12. Ibid., 393–94.

13. Arthur M. Schlesinger, Jr., *The Age of Jackson* (Boston: Little, Brown & Co., 1945), 293.

14. David C. Whitney, *The American Presidents* (Garden City, N.Y.: Doubleday, 1967), 102.

15. Charles Richard Williams, ed., *The Diary and Letters of Rutherford B. Hayes*, 5 vols. (Columbus, Ohio: Ohio State Archaeological and Historical Society, 1922–26) 3:644–45.

16. Asa E. Martin, *After the White House* (University Park: Pennsylvania State University Press, 1951), 306.

17. Edmund Fuller and David E. Green, *God in the White House* (New York: Crown, 1968), 162. Ironically, this most muscular of Christians — who had earlier stirred controversy by labeling Thomas Paine a "filthy little atheist" — incurred charges of faithlessness himself when he tried to remove the words "In God We Trust" from the nation's currency. Roosevelt believed the phrase both sacrilegious and unconstitutional.

18. A magazine of the era captured Roosevelt's egotism as well as his irresistible news value when it celebrated "The Scrapes He Gets Into, the Scrapes He Gets Out Of; the Things He Attempts, the Things He Accomplishes; His Appointments and His Disappointments; the Rebukes that He Administers and Those He Receives; His Assumptions, Presumptions, Omniscience and Deficiencies, Make Up a Daily Tale Which Those of Us Who Survive His Tenure of the President's Office Will Doubtless Miss, as We Might Miss Some Property of the Atmosphere We Breathe," Gardner, *Departing Glory*, 70.

"I always believe in going hard at everything," said TR, which explained the president's Tennis Cabinet and hundred-mile horseback rides through the Virginia countryside — the latter an annoyance to a military establishment woefully out of shape and none too grateful for the presidential reminder. In foreign affairs, Rooseveltian pugnacity was responsible for the Panama Canal and the global voyage of the Great White Fleet. Less auspiciously, it also produced TR's dismissal of Czar Nicholas as "a preposterous little creature," which was hardly worse than the epithets ("circumcised skunk," "copper riveted idiot") the president bestowed on his domestic enemies.

19. Elizabeth Frost, ed., *The Bully Pulpit: Quotations from America's Presidents* (New York: Facts on File, 1988), 182.

20. Ellen Wilson was not alone in her reaction. Wrote the *New York Times*, "The wonder is that in seven years Theodore Roosevelt never thought of this way of stamping his personality upon the age." John Tebbel and Sarah Miles Watts, *The Press and the Presidency* (New York: Oxford University Press, 1985), 379.

21. Courtly if unpersuaded, Wilson wished to invite one freezing group of suffragists inside the White House for some hot tea. "It's cold out there," he remarked to his implacable second wife, Edith. Eventually, head usher Ike Hoover was dispatched, over the First Lady's protests, to extend an offer of presidential hospitality. The demonstrators rejected Wilson's overture, and were sentenced to fifteen days in jail for disturbing the peace. Lillian Rogers Parks, *My Thirty Years Backstairs at the White House* (New York: Fleet Publishing, 1961), 150.

22. Ibid., 152.

23. Bailey, *Presidential Greatness*, 201. Adams's famous prayer reads as follows: "I pray Heaven to bestow the best of blessings on this house and all that shall hereafter inhabit it. May none but wise and honest men ever rule under this roof."

24. Fred I. Greenstein, ed., *Leadership in the Modern Presidency* (Cambridge: Harvard University Press, 1988), 19. Walter Johnson, *1600 Pennsylvania Avenue: Presidents and the People, 1929–1959* (Boston: Little, Brown & Co., 1960), 189. As Johnson points out, FDR was fortunate in his timing: 1935 saw the birth of AP's wirephoto service, while the next two years witnessed the first editions of the hugely successful *Life* and *Look*.

25. Richard Norton Smith, *Thomas E. Dewey and His Times* (New York: Simon & Schuster, 1982), 398.

26. Smith, *An Uncommon Man*, 111.

27. Myra Greenberg Gutin, "The President's Partner: The First Lady as Public Communicator, 1920–1976" (Ph.D. diss., University of Michigan, 1983), 356–60. (Since published as *The President's Partner: The First Lady in the Twentieth Century* [Westport, Conn.: Greenwood Press, 1989]). As shrewd in her press relations as her husband, Mrs. Roosevelt told a reporter for the *New York Herald Tribune* that she deliberately flouted the journalistic conventions of Washington. Acknowledging that some of the things she said might be kept off the record by a more cautious politician, the First Lady added, "What you don't understand is that perhaps I am making these statements on purpose to arouse controversy and thereby get the topics talked about and so get people to thinking about

them." Joseph P. Lash, *Eleanor and Franklin* (New York: W. W. Norton & Co., 1971), 363.

28. Mrs. Roosevelt earned $500 per minute — and criticism to match — for radio appearances sponsored by the likes of Simmons Mattress Company and Sweetheart Soap. In 1933 alone, she received 300,000 pieces of mail, and was heard more often by America's radio audience than was the president. Hitler's comment about Mrs. Roosevelt's alleged supremacy is in Carl Sferrazza Anthony's *First Ladies: The Saga of the Presidents' Wives and Their Power, 1789–1961* (New York: William Morrow, 1990), 485.

29. Merriman Smith, *Merriman Smith's Book of Presidents: A White House Memoir*, ed. Timothy G. Smith (New York: W. W. Norton & Co., 1972), 50.

30. Greenstein, *Leadership in the Modern Presidency*, 105.

31. Rowland Evans, Jr., and Robert Novak, *Nixon in the White House: The Frustration of Power* (New York: Random House, 1971), 233–37.

32. George C. Edwards III, *The Public Presidency: The Pursuit of Popular Support* (New York: St. Martin's Press, 1983), 77–78.

33. Robert E. Denton, Jr., and Dan F. Hohn, *Presidential Communication* (New York: Praeger, 1986), 61.

34. Edwards, *The Public Presidency*, 82.

35. Transcript of "LBJ," broadcast September 23, 1992, PBS.

36. Liz Carpenter, *Ruffles and Flourishes* (Garden City, N.Y.: Doubleday, 1970), 32.

4

"This Damned Old House":

The Lincolns
in the White House

David Herbert Donald

Shortly after Abraham Lincoln was inaugurated president in 1861, an old friend from Illinois asked him how he liked living in the Executive Mansion (as the White House was generally called in those days). Lincoln replied that he felt a bit like the reprobate in Springfield who had been tarred and feathered and ridden out of town on a rail. If it wasn't for the honor of it, he said, he'd much rather have walked.[1] That wry, detached attitude was to serve Lincoln well during his four years in the White House. It was, unfortunately, not an attitude that his wife, Mary Todd Lincoln, could share.

I

When the Lincolns moved into the White House on March 4, 1861, they were less prepared than any previous occupants for the duties and challenges they would have to face. An able Illinois lawyer who had gained a national reputation in his debates with Stephen A. Douglas, Lincoln, at the age of fifty-two, had no administrative experience of any sort; he had never been governor of his state or even mayor of his town of Springfield. A profound student of the Constitution and of the writings of the

Founding Fathers, he had a limited acquaintance with the government that they had established. He had served only a single, rather unsuccessful term in the House of Representatives in the 1840s and had not returned to the national capital since. Though Lincoln was one of the founders of the Republican party, he had few acquaintances and almost no close personal friends in Washington. In charge of the country's foreign relations, he had no correspondents abroad and no acquaintance with any ruler of a foreign nation.

Nearly a decade younger than her husband, Mary Lincoln was equally unprepared to be mistress of the White House. The daughter of a well-to-do merchant and cotton manufacturer, she had grown up in comfort in Lexington, Kentucky, where she had received the best education available for young women — including instruction in French. But for the previous twenty-five years, she had lived in semi-frontier Illinois, with only an occasional visit to her Kentucky relatives and one unhappy winter in Washington when her husband was in Congress. In a modest frame house on Eighth Street in Springfield, she had made a comfortable middle-class home for her husband and their children. Like her husband, she had no friends in Washington.

Clearly, had the Lincolns occupied the Executive Mansion during the most tranquil of times they would have faced difficulties. But in 1861 the circumstances were particularly trying. The states of the Deep South had seceded and set up the Confederate States of America. While Confederate troops besieged Fort Sumter in Charleston Harbor, one of the few installations in the South still in Union hands, the states of the Upper South teetered between union and secession. Lincoln had to face this crisis as the first Republican president, obliged to create an administration from discordant groups that had never before worked together. Even as Lincoln was sworn into office, members of his party were beating on the doors of the White House demanding that the spoils of office be distributed to the party faithful. Hounded by office seekers, Lincoln said he sometimes felt like a hotel keeper who was trying to put out a fire in one wing of his establishment while renting rooms in another.

Mary Lincoln's problems were equally severe. Because she was the wife of a Republican — who completely supported her husband's views and ambitions — the Southern women who dominated Washington society resolved to snub her. The few New England women in the national capital distrusted her because she was Southern-born and because, eventually, four of her brothers and three of her brothers-in-law enlisted in the Confederate army. Easterners in general were sure that she was an uncouth frontier woman — doubtless as uneducated as an Indian squaw, and smoking a corncob pipe. Whatever she did — or failed to do — was certain to be closely watched and criticized.

It was, then, with trepidation that the Lincolns on the morning after the inauguration began to explore the Executive Mansion. They were overwhelmed by the size of their new residence with its thirty-one rooms, not including the conservatory, various outbuildings, and stables. The East Room alone was about as large as their entire Springfield house. After a quick inspection, Lincoln, who was totally indifferent to his physical surroundings, concluded that the mansion was in good shape, and was ready to settle down to work. But Mrs. Lincoln came up with a very different verdict. Accompanied by her sisters, who were visiting her from Springfield, she went from room to room, finding the furniture broken down, the wallpaper peeling, the carpeting worn, the draperies torn, the eleven basement rooms filthy and rat-infested; the whole place had the air of a run-down, unsuccessful, third-rate hotel.[2]

Both the Lincolns promptly discovered that the Executive Mansion was as much a public building as it was a home. Except for the family dining rooms, all the rooms on the first floor were open to all visitors, and anybody who wanted to could stroll in at any hour of the day and often late at night. A single elderly doorkeeper was supposed to prevent depredations, but often no one was on duty.[3]

On the second floor, nearly half of the rooms were also public; they were devoted to the business of the chief executive. Here were a reception room, the offices of the president's secretary, and the president's own office, which also served as the cabinet room. A solid black walnut table occupied the center of the president's office. Along one wall of the room were a sofa and two upholstered chairs, above which hung maps of the theaters of military operations. In a corner by the window was a large upright mahogany desk, so battered that one of Lincoln's secretaries thought it must have come "from some old furniture auction"; the pigeonholes above it served as a filing cabinet. Lincoln's smaller working desk stood between the two windows.[4] All the furnishings of this wing of the White House were of the most nondescript kind, and the floor was mostly covered with oilcloth, which made it easier to clean up after overflowing or missed spittoons.

From early morning until dusk, these rooms were thronged with senators, congressmen, applicants for government jobs, candidates for military appointments, foreign dignitaries, and plain citizens who had favors to ask or who just wanted to shake their president's hand. In the early months of Lincoln's first administration, the line was often so long that it extended down the stairs to the front entrance, with a candidate for a job or a military appointment perched on each step. Lincoln found himself a prisoner in his own office; every time he stepped out into the corridor to go to the family quarters on the west end of the corridor, he was besieged with complaints and petitions. Finally, in order to gain a little privacy, he ordered the only structural addition made to the White House during his administration — a partition built through the reception room, which allowed him to retreat unobserved from his office into the family's private rooms.

Those private quarters, which initially seemed so palatial, proved to be remarkably constricted. There were, in fact, only six or seven rooms where the Lincolns could enjoy any privacy. They made the upstairs oval room the family sitting room. The two adjoining rooms on the south side were those of President and Mrs. Lincoln; as in Springfield, they used separate, but connecting, bedrooms. Across the wide corridor were the "Prince of Wales Room," the state guest room of the Executive Mansion, and the infrequently used room of their oldest son, Robert Todd Lincoln, a student at Harvard College, who was in the White House only during brief vacation periods; the rest of the time it served as a guest room.[5] Also on the north side were the rooms of the two youngest Lincoln boys — Willie, aged ten, and Thomas (always called "Tad"), who was eight.

II

The two younger Lincoln boys found endless opportunities for adventure and mischief in the Executive Mansion. Adults saw the soldiers stationed on the south grounds of the White House as an ominous re-

The Lincoln family in a stylized portrait. Although the Lincoln family never sat together for an artist, prints such as this received wide circulation. Courtesy of the White House.

minder of danger, but to Willie and Tad the members of the "Bucktail" Pennsylvania regiment were playmates who could always be counted on for stories and races. Catching the martial spirit, Willie and Tad took great pleasure in drilling all the neighborhood boys they could round up. With two special friends who just matched them in age — Bud and Holly Taft, children of a federal judge who lived nearby — they commandeered the roof of the mansion for their fort, and here, with small logs painted to look like cannon, they resolutely fired away at unseen Confederates across the Potomac. Intensely patriotic, Willie published a poem in the Washington *National Republican* about the heroic death of a friend at Ball's Bluff. Tad, a little less clear about what was going on, managed to create a sensation when his father was solemnly reviewing Union troops on Pennsylvania Avenue by slipping in behind the president and waving a Confederate flag.[6]

Children in the White House were something new for Americans, and citizens began showering them with presents. The most valued, and the most lasting, were the pets. Someone presented to Willie a beautiful little pony, to which he was devoted; he rode the animal nearly every day and, being a generous boy, often allowed Tad to ride, even though the younger boy was so small that his legs stuck straight out on the sides. Especially cherished were two small goats, Nanko and Nannie, which frisked on the White House grounds and, when they had an opportunity, wrought destruction in the White House garden. But they were not entirely outside animals; like the public at large, they had the run of the White House. On one occasion Tad harnessed Nanko up to a chair, which served as a sled, and drove triumphantly through the East Room, where a reception was in progress. As dignified matrons held up their hoop skirts, Nanko pulled the yelling boy around the room and out through the door again.[7]

When Lincoln could, he played with his boys. One day Julia Taft, the teen-aged sister of Bud and Holly, heard a great commotion in the upstairs oval room and, entering, found the president of the United States lying on his back on the floor, Willie and Bud holding down his arms, Tad and Holly, his legs. "Julie, come quick and sit on his stomach!" cried Tad, as the president grinned at her grandly. There were also quiet times, when Lincoln told stories or read to the boys; he would balance

Willie and Bud on each knee, while Tad mounted on the back of his big chair and Holly climbed on the arm.[8]

But during his first year in office, Lincoln had all too little time for his sons, for he was busy learning his job. The Department of State sent over a detailed memorandum of the clothing that a president was expected to wear. Obediently, Lincoln followed directions, though, with his ungainly figure and his immense height, his coat always seemed rumpled and his cravat askew. His huge hands, enlarged by years of plowing and splitting rails, were never comfortable in the white kid gloves that the State Department prescribed; once, holding up his hands encased in a new pair of these gloves, he said they looked like canvased hams.

In the first days of his administration he tried to be orderly and businesslike. For instance, he began by trying to scan and digest all the morning papers that reached the White House. Finding that too time-consuming, he instructed his secretaries to prepare a digest of the news for his perusal, but presently he discontinued even that. Though occasionally he glanced at the telegraphic news despatches in one or two papers, he read none of the papers consistently and almost never looked at their editorials. There was, he concluded, nothing that newspapermen could tell him that he did not already know.

After the early days of the administration, much of Lincoln's mail received no closer attention than did the newspapers. To assist the chief executive, the Congress had provided a staff of only one secretary. Since even the methodical young German, John G. Nicolay, whom Lincoln appointed to this office, could not begin to handle all the work, the president was allowed, in effect, to borrow two additional clerks from other offices of the government.[9] A principal duty of these three young men was to screen the president's mail — some two hundred or three hundred letters a day. Scores of these were requests for information or applications for jobs that could readily be referred to the cabinet departments. Dozens of other letters they simply threw into the wastebasket: crank letters, threatening letters, letters containing messages from supernatural powers, letters soliciting the president's endorsement of commercial schemes. The rest, which the secretaries carefully endorsed on the back with the name of the writer and a brief indication of the contents, had to be seen and answered by the president himself. To many of these he replied in his own handwriting, often taking the time to make a careful copy of his response for his files. Then letters and answers were filed away in the pigeonholes above the president's desk.

Lincoln worked long hours at his desk. Much of his time was taken in receiving the hundreds of candidates, applicants, petitioners, suppliants, and visitors who wanted to see him. Most of these he handled expeditiously, quickly scanning letters of recommendation and referring them to the proper authorities, listening intently to complaints and making proper sympathetic noises. Whenever possible he avoided flatly rejecting an application for help, preferring to tell one of his celebrated "leetle stories" to suggest the unreasonableness of the request. For instance, when an officer accused of embezzling forty dollars of government money appealed for leniency on the ground that he had really stolen only thirty dollars, Lincoln was reminded of an Indiana man who charged his neighbor's daughter with unseemly behavior for having three illegitimate children. "'Now,' said the man whose family was so outrageously scandalized, 'that's a lie, and I can prove it, for she only has two.'"[10]

Lincoln's friends worried that he was confined to his office so much of the time and urged him to get fresh air and take exercise, but the president insisted upon seeing everybody who wanted to see him. "They do not want much, and they get very little," he said. "I know how I would feel in their place."[11]

Remarkably, during Lincoln's first year in office, the president's systematic lack of system seemed to work. Stories of his patience, his humanity, his accessibility to even the humblest petitioner spread throughout the North. Millions referred to him as Father Abraham — though, in fact, he was one of the youngest men elected president. For the first time in American history, citizens began to feel that the occupant of the White Hosue was *their* representative, and they showered him with gifts: a firkin of butter, a crate of Bartlett pears, New England salmon. With special appropriateness a man from Johnsburgh, New York, sent Lincoln "a live American Eagle[,] the bird of our land," which had lost one foot in a trap. "But," the New Yorker continued, "he is yet an Eagle and perhaps no more cripled [*sic*] than the Nation whose banner he represented; his wings are sound and will extend seven feet."[12]

In part the common people rallied behind the new president because, in time of war, most Americans support their government. They were content to give the new administration a chance to find itself. Even the disaster to Union troops at the battle of Bull Run in July 1861 did little to abate this willingness. And by the beginning of 1862 it appeared that the Lincoln government was beginning to be master of the situation. In the West, General Ulysses S. Grant broke the Confederate line at Forts Henry and Donelson and most of Tennessee fell into Union hands. In the South, Commodore David G. Farragut captured New Orleans. On the seaboard, Union amphibious teams established a foothold on the Sea Islands of South Carolina and had control of Cape Hatteras in North Carolina. And in the East, General George B. McClellan had recruited, organized, and drilled the finest army ever seen on the American continent, which seemed poised to capture Richmond. It was little wonder that by early spring Lincoln's mail was filled with letters like one from retired General Winfield Scott rejoicing in "the inevitable and early suppression of the Great American rebellion."[13]

Meanwhile, during these same twelve months, Mrs. Lincoln was achieving some successes of her own. Indeed, she became the most conspicuous female occupant of the Executive Mansion since Dolley Madison. Brought up to express an active interest in public affairs, deeply involved in her husband's political career, Mary Lincoln had no intention of fading quietly into the background in Washington. She intended to become, and was, the First Lady of the land — a term that was coined to describe her.

She made it her main project to refurbish the White House. Congress had appropriated $20,000 to be expended over the four years of her husband's term of office for the rehabilitation of the Executive Mansion. This was, to her, an immense amount of money — worth at least ten times as much in present-day purchasing power; it was more than four times the Lincoln family's total income in the average year before 1860. To Mary it seemed an infinite treasure.

She went to New York and Philadelphia in order to buy furnishings suitable for the mansion of the president of the United States and his

First Lady. Merchants welcomed her with open arms, showing her the best and most expensive carpeting, material for upholstery and drapes, furniture, and china. She bought everything. Much of her effort went into making the upstairs living quarters homey and comfortable. She took special pains with the guest bedroom, repapering it with light purple wallpaper figured with gold roses. For this room she ordered the ornately carved seven-foot rosewood bed that has since been known as the "Lincoln bed," though in fact the president probably never slept in it. It was framed in the most elegant of canopies, made of purple silk trimmed with gold lace gathered together at the headboard in a gold coronet. But most of her purchases were for the public room downstairs. The receipted bills in the National Achives show that she purchased chairs, sofas, and hassocks; fabrics of damask, brocade, pink tarlatan, plush, and "French Satin DeLaine"; wallpaper imported from France; and a full set of Haviland china in "Solferino and gold," with the American coat of arms in the center of each plate. For the Red Room she ordered 117 yards of crimson Wilton carpet; and for the East Room, an imported Brussels velvet carpet, pale green in color, ingeniously woven as a single piece,[14] which, one admirer gushed, "in effect looked as if the ocean, in gleaming and transparent waves, were tossing roses at your feet."[15]

Returning to Washington, she personally oversaw the scrubbing, painting, and plastering of the entire White House, so that for the first time in years the Executive Mansion was sparklingly clean. As her new furnishings began to arrive, the whole place took on a look of elegance. To modern eyes Mary Lincoln's fondness for ornate laces, for heavy, tasseled drapes, for plush, overstuffed furniture seems at best quaint and at worst vulgar; but this was the height of the Victorian age, when less was certainly not more. Even critical observers were impressed by her accomplishment.

But then, inevitably, the bills began coming in. In December 1861 she discovered that she had exceeded the congressional appropriation by $6,700. She sought desperately to hide her extravagance from her husband, arguing — quite correctly — that such overruns were common in governmental expenditures and that this deficit could easily be concealed by a little budget-juggling. Finally, she was obliged to ask the Commissioner of Public Buildings, who kept the White House accounts, to explain the situation to the president and to ask him to sponsor a supplemental congressional appropriation.

Lincoln was furious. He would never, he said, endorse such a deficiency appropriation. "It would stink in the nostrils of the American people to have it said that the President of the United States had approved a bill overrunning an appropriation of $20 000 for *flub dubs* for this damned old house, when the soldiers cannot have blankets." "It was all wrong to spend one cent at such a time," he went on, "and I never ought to have had a cent expended; the house was furnished well enough, better than any one we ever lived in."[16] Rather than ask Congress for more money, he vowed to pay for Mary's purchases out of his own pocket. Eventually, though, he was obliged to recede from his position, and Congress quietly passed two deficiency appropriations to cover Mary Lincoln's expenditures.

With that obstacle overcome, Mary Lincoln was ready to celebrate her success, and on February 5, 1862, she held a reception, with admission limited to five hundred invited guests, rather than being open to the public at large. Inevitably, there was much grumbling among those who were not invited. Carriages began arriving about nine in the evening with besworded, overdecorated diplomats, generals in bright uniforms, members of the cabinet, Supreme Court justices, and selected senators and congressmen. In the East Room they were greeted by the president, who was wearing a black swallowtail coat, and the First Lady, whose white silk dress, decorated with hundreds of small black flowers, exposed a remarkably low décolletage. In the background the United States Marine Band played, its repertoire including a sprightly new piece, "The Mary Lincoln Polka." At midnight the doors to the dining room were opened to reveal a magnificent buffet concocted by Maillard's of New York, which displayed sugary models of the Ship of State, Fort Sumter, and Fort Pickens flanked by mounds of turkey, duck, ham, terrapin, and pheasant. Dinner was served until three, and many guests stayed till daybreak. Altogether, concluded the *Washington Star*, the reception was "the most superb affair of its kind ever seen here."[17]

Peter Frederick Rothermel's 1867 painting *The Republican Court in the Days of Lincoln* provides a sense of the receptions at which Lincoln, like most nineteenth-century chief executives, spent time fulfilling the social obligations of his office. Courtesy of the White House.

III

That February 1862 party marked a turning point in the Lincolns' life in the White House. Even while the visitors downstairs were celebrating Mary Lincoln's refurbishing of the Executive Mansion and Abraham Lincoln's prospective victory over the Confederacy, upstairs the two small Lincoln boys were desperately ill with "bilious fever" — probably typhoid fever, caused by pollution in the White House water system. Deeply anxious, their parents had considered canceling the grand reception, but the family doctor assured them that the boys were in no immediate danger. Even so, both the president and his wife quietly slipped upstairs during the celebration to be at their sons' bedsides. During the next two weeks, Tad continued to be very ill, but Willie grew worse and worse. On Thursday, February 20, he died.

Both parents were prostrated with grief. Lincoln had loved this cheerful, intelligent boy probably more than any of his other children, and he found it difficult to accept his loss. Though he had to go through the motions of continuing the business of the presidency, his heart was not in it. But slowly he came to identify the loss of Willie with that of so many other young Americans who were dying from disease or battle, and his private grief became the source for an even greater resolution to preserve the Union.

His wife could not so sublimate her grief. Having earlier lost a favorite son, Eddie, in Springfield, Mary Lincoln could not deal with this second death, and for three weeks she took to her bed, so desolated that she could not attend the funeral or look after Tad, who was slowly beginning to recover. For many months the mere mention of Willie's name was enough to send her into paroxysms of weeping, and it was necessary for Lincoln to employ a nurse to look after her. Never again did Mary Lincoln enter the bedroom where Willie had died, nor the downstairs Green Room, where his body had been embalmed. When she was finally able to emerge from her room, Mary Lincoln went into such profound mourning dress that she was almost invisible under the layers of black veils and crepes.

In these circumstances, of course, all social activities at the White House ceased, as the Executive Mansion was heavily draped in black.

Grieving over the death of her son, Mary Lincoln gave little further thought to the mansion that she had so tastefully redecorated, and in the months following Willie's death, while the public rooms were largely unattended and unoccupied, an enormous amount of vandalism occurred. Souvenir hunters managed to steal yard-long swatches of the drapes and carpets and to cut out the delicate medallions from the lace curtains.

But such material concerns were no longer of much interest to Mary Lincoln, who sought to reach out to Willie beyond the grave. Presently she became the victim of spiritualists, who claimed they could put her in touch with her darling lost boy. Often she went to a medium's darkened chambers, but on eight occasions séances were held in the White House itself. The president attended at least one of these, not out of any belief in spiritualism, but in a desire to see who was preying on his wife's mental instability.[18]

It would, however, have been difficult to blame President Lincoln had he sought any kind of supernatural help at this time, since his own successes seemed as transient as Mary Lincoln's. By mid-1862 it was clear that the anticipated Union victory in the Civil War was not coming about. In the western theater, after the bloody battle of Shiloh, the Union armies were stalled. In the East, the Army of the Potomac got within sight of Richmond but then was driven back. With his grand strategy crumbling, Lincoln desperately sought new commanders who could bring quick victories. In a game of military musical chairs, General John Pope took command and brought about the Union defeat at Second Bull Run; Ambrose P. Burnside led in the fiasco at Fredericksburg; boastful Joseph Hooker brought about the rout at Chancellorsville. With military defeats came political rebuffs. Invoking military necessity, Lincoln issued his Emancipation Proclamation, which contributed to the defeat of the Republican party in the congressional elections of 1862. So inept was Lincoln thought to be that in December 1862 a caucus of the leaders of his own party in the Senate urged him to fire his secretary of state and reconstruct his whole cabinet.

Though shaken, the president applied himself to the duties of his office with a grim intensity that helped distract him from his personal woes. Rising early after a generally sleepless night, Lincoln went at once to his desk, where he worked for an hour or so before breakfast, which consisted of a cup of coffee and an egg. He returned to his office to examine papers and sign commissions for another hour or so until ten o'clock, when public petitioners were allowed in. At one o'clock — unless he forgot about it — he took a brief break for lunch with Mary and Tad and occasionally a close family friend; abstemious as always, he customarily ate only an apple and drank a glass of milk. Then he went back to the office, where he remained for most of the afternoon, unless he could be persuaded to take a horseback or carriage ride. Having no interest in food, he ate a spartan dinner, with no alcohol, and unless there was some ceremony or reception that required his presence, he once again went back to his desk. Late at night he would frequently walk alone through the White House grounds to the War Department to read the latest telegraphic despatches from the armies. Only then, if there was no major fighting underway, did he feel he could relax for a few minutes with his family. "I consider myself fortunate," Mary Lincoln wrote at this time, "if at eleven o'clock, I once more find myself, in my pleasant room and very especially, if my tired and weary Husband is *there*, waiting in the lounge to receive me."[19]

Inevitably, with such a schedule, President and Mrs. Lincoln began to drift apart. For some time the Lincolns had slept in separate, but adjoining, bedrooms; now, after the death of Willie, Tad was so lonely and so subject to nightmares that he was regularly allowed to sleep in his father's bed. Mary Lincoln was totally absorbed in her own affairs and in her grief. Lincoln, of course, was aware of his wife's unstable condition, but nobody knew how such mental illness should be treated. In any case, he was desperately exhausted. Always thin, he had now lost so much weight as to look cadaverous. Though worn out, he managed to keep his sense of humor about his appearance; when somebody told him he was "thin as a shad," he responded — in an atrocious pun — that he looked even "worse — as thin as a shadder."[20] Great black circles ringed his eyes. Chronically weary, he was never able to get any rest; as he expressed it, the little relaxation he allowed himself "seemed never to reach the *tired* spot."[21]

Coming to regard the White House as a prison, both the Lincolns were happy to escape during the summer months to a cottage on the grounds

A rare tranquil moment for Abraham Lincoln with his son Tad is shown in this portrait by Francis Bicknell Carpenter. As was customary in nineteenth-century American portraits, the scene in the background identifies the subject's occupation. Courtesy of the White House.

of the Soldiers' Home, three miles north of Washington. But presidential duties continued without interruption, and Lincoln rode or drove back and forth to his office every day. Nor did Mary Lincoln's anxieties abate. She was often in a state of near-hysteria concerning her husband's safety — and with reason, because on one occasion when Lincoln was riding to the White House, a stray bullet, whether from a would-be assassin or an overzealous soldier, penetrated his hat. Mary had an additional source of worry because her oldest son, Robert, about to graduate from Harvard, wanted to enlist in the Union army. He had the tacit approval of his father, but she frantically and obdurately opposed it, saying that she had already sacrificed one son to the Union cause and could not spare another.

IV

A year after Willie's death, Mary Lincoln emerged from full mourning, and the endless round of White House entertainment began again. Hardly a week passed without one or two state dinners at the White House — for the diplomatic corps, for visiting foreign dignitaries, for congressmen. Every week there were two evening receptions, one on Tuesday and the other on Saturday. At eight o'clock guests were admitted at the North Portico and crossed the broad corridor to the Red Room. There the master of ceremonies — usually Ward Hill Lamon, an old Illinois friend who was now marshal of the District of Columbia — introduced them to the president, who shook each guest's hand, even though by the end of one of these evenings his own hands were usually raw with blisters. They were then presented to Mrs. Lincoln, who was saved from having to shake hands because her hoop skirts made it impossible for anyone to approach closer than three feet. They were next shepherded through the Green Room into the great East Room, where they stood about and talked; no food or drink was served. At ten o'clock the president, with Mrs. Lincoln on his arm, entered and made a circuit of the room, the U.S. Marine Band played "Hail Columbia," and the party was over.[22]

These social affairs were exhausting to the tired president and his distraught wife. Bored and depressed, the Lincolns were not at their best on these occasions. Coming away from a reception, Richard Henry

Dana, Jr., reported that "Mrs. Lincoln looks like the housekeeper of the establishment, and a notable, prying and not goodtempered housekeeper," while "'Abe' looks like a man who has brought in something to sell."[23] Aware of such criticisms, both Lincolns believed such social functions were necessary to maintain morale in time of war. Anyway, the president claimed these thousands of visitors were valuable to him; they gave him a "public opinion bath," a better way of understanding what ordinary citizens were thinking and saying.

By this time Mary Lincoln had largely abandoned her efforts to impress Washington society, and she now devoted her limited energy to visiting the wounded Union soldiers in the army hospitals around Washington, bringing them flowers from the White House conservatory and offering comfort and advice. She also took a special interest in the camps of "contrabands," former slaves who had congregated in the District of Columbia, often without housing, food, or elementary medical facilities. Unfortunately for her reputation, she failed to take a friendly newspaper correspondent or two along with her on these expeditions of mercy, and they went largely unnoticed by a public daily made aware of her increasingly eccentric behavior.

She began to travel a good deal, usually accompanied by Tad. There were trips to New York, to Long Branch, New Jersey, to Boston to see Robert, and to the White Mountains. And everywhere she went, she gratified her passion for shopping; once directed toward refitting the White House, it was now indulged to outfit her person. She could not check her desire to buy; she needed a $1,500 cashmere shawl, she needed new dresses, she needed specially made hats, she needed gloves — indeed, it was said that she purchased no fewer than four hundred pairs of gloves in a three-month period. Her passion for material possessions became boundless. When the Lincoln family — all three members — moved to the Soldiers' Home for the summer of 1863, she required a train of nineteen wagons to haul out the necessary supplies and clothing.

Though Mary Lincoln was not by this point entirely rational, there was a kind of logic — to be sure, a circular logic — behind her obsessive concern for clothing. She knew that she was accumulating huge debts, but she thought a failure to dress in proper style would cause people to turn against her husband and result in his defeat in the 1864 presidential election. "If he is re-elected, I can keep him in ignorance of my affairs," she thought, "but if he is defeated, then the bills will be sent in, and he will know all."[24]

Though proud of his wife's handsome appearance, the president, it is certain, never thought of Mary Lincoln's expensive dresses as a factor in his reelection. Much more important in his mind was the continued failure of the Union armies to achieve victory on the battlefield. In mid-1863 Union successes at Vicksburg and Gettysburg roused Northern hopes, but neither victory was followed by further decisive action. The following year Grant, brought East as commander in chief of all the Union armies, led a series of direct assaults on Confederate armies which by mid-year brought him no closer to Richmond than McClellan had been two years earlier. War-weariness among civilians and desertion among soldiers were rampant, and the Democrats nominated General McClellan for president on a platform that promised peace. So dispiriting was the outlook that Lincoln glumly predicted his own defeat in the 1864 election.

Then the tide turned. General William T. Sherman's capture of Atlanta came just in time to cheer Union supporters throughout the North, and Lincoln was reelected. Shortly afterward, as Sherman blazed a track of destruction across Georgia and Grant gained a stranglehold on Richmond, it became clear that the Confederacy was doomed. Night after night the White House was illuminated to celebrate Union victories, and crowds gathered on the North Lawn to serenade the president and to hear a few words from him about the successes Union arms were achieving.

Life in the White House during these final weeks of the conflict achieved a tranquillity that the Lincolns had not hitherto known. With all the major decisions made, with the armies admirably commanded, the president no longer had to feel personally responsible for every action or to sit up nights waiting in the telegraph room of the War Department for news of the latest disaster. Aware that there were still severe political problems, he tried to get some rest. He made a point of taking Mary and Tad on several little jaunts, ostensibly to inspect the armies, but in fact to secure a respite from his daily routine.

As the end of the war approached, both Lincolns felt they were awakening from what Mary called "this hideous nightmare" through which they had been living. On Friday, April 14, 1865, the president seemed particularly happy. "Dear husband," Mary remarked, "you almost startle me, by your great cheerfulness." That afternoon they took a carriage ride, and the president, "cheerful — . . . even playful," talked of the happier times ahead of them. "Mary," he said, "I consider *this day*, the war has come to a close. — We must *both*, be more cheerful in the future — between the war & the loss of our darling Willie — we have both, been very miserable."[25] By the time they returned to the White House, Mary was beginning to have one of her headaches and thought of staying at home for the evening. But Lincoln had already given his word that he would appear in the presidential box at the popular Ford's Theater. Mary put on a pretty bonnet and a small-patterned blue dress, and he got ready by brushing his hair with his hand and picking up his silk hat. Arm in arm they went out the north door of the White House for the last time together.

N O T E S

1. J. G. Randall, *Lincoln the President: Midstream* (New York: Dodd, Mead & Co., 1952), 2.

2. For a full and valuable account of the Lincolns in the White House, see William Seale, *The President's House: A History* (Washington: White House Historical Association, 1986), chaps. 15–17.

3. On White House security, see William A. Croffut, "Lincoln's Washington: Recollections of a Journalist Who Knew Everybody," *Atlantic Monthly* 145 (January 1930): 64.

4. William O. Stoddard, *Inside the White House in War Times* (New York: Charles L. Webster & Co., 1890), 23–24. Cf. the drawing C. L. Stellwagen made of Lincoln's office in October 1864, in White House Historical Association, *The White House: An Historical Guide* (Washington: White House Historical Association, 1963), 128.

5. For a diagram showing the public and private rooms on the second floor, see Seale, *The President's House*, 394 ff.

6. For an engaging account of the Lincoln children in the White House, see Ruth Painter Randall, *Lincoln's Sons* (Boston: Little, Brown & Co., 1955).

7. On the pets in the Lincoln household, see Ruth Painter Randall, *Lincoln's Animal Friends* (Boston: Little, Brown & Co., 1958).

8. Julia Taft Bayne, *Tad Lincoln's Father* (Boston: Little, Brown & Co., 1931), 108, 110.

9. On Nicolay and the administration of the president's office, see Helen Nicolay, *Lincoln's Secretary: A Biography of John G. Nicolay* (New York: Longmans, Green and Co., 1949). See also Edward D. Neill, *Abraham Lincoln and His Mailbag* (St. Paul: Minnesota Historical Society, 1964), 46–50.

10. Ward Hill Lamon, *Recollections of Abraham Lincoln, 1847–1865*, ed. Dorothy Lamon Teillard (Washington, 1911), 82–83.

11. Benjamin P. Thomas, *Abraham Lincoln: A Biography* (New York: Alfred A. Knopf, 1952), 457.

12. D. M. Jenks to Abraham Lincoln, June 10, 1862, Abraham Lincoln Manuscripts, Library of Congress.

13. Winfield Scott to W. H. Seward, April 28, 1862, Lincoln MSS.

14. On these purchases, see Ruth Painter Randall, *Mary Lincoln: Biography of a Marriage* (Boston: Little, Brown & Co., 1953), 260–61.

15. Mary Clemmer Ames, *Ten Years in Washington* (Hartford, Conn.: A. D. Worthington & Co., 1873), 171–72.

16. Ruth P. Randall, *Mary Lincoln*, 264–65. Cf. Benjamin Brown French, *Witness to the Young Republic*, ed. Donald B. Cole and John J. McDonough (Hanover, N.H.: University Press of New England, 1989), 382.

17. For an elaborate account of this reception, together with a wood engraving of the scene, see *Frank Leslie's Illustrated Newspaper* 13 (February 22, 1862): 209–10, 213–14. Marie D. Smith, *Entertaining in the White House* (Washington: Acropolis Books, 1967), 102, gives the menu.

18. For a sympathetic presentation of Mary Lincoln's interest in spiritualism, see Jean Harvey Baker, *Mary Todd Lincoln: A Biography* (New York: W. W. Norton & Co., 1987), 214–22.

19. Justin G. Turner and Linda Levitt Turner, *Mary Todd Lincoln: Her Life and Letters* (New York: Alfred A. Knopf, 1972), 187.

20. J. G. Randall, *Lincoln the President: Midstream*, 64.

21. Francis B. Carpenter, *The Inner Life of Abraham Lincoln: Six Months at the White House* (Boston: Houghton, Osgood and Co., 1879), 217.

22. Stoddard, *Inside the White House*, 96–97.

23. Richard Henry Dana, Jr., Diary, January 7, 1862, Dana Manuscripts, Massachusetts Historical Society.

24. Elizabeth Keckley, *Behind the Scenes: Thirty Years a Slave and Four Years in the White House* (New York: Arno Press, 1968), 150.

25. Carl Sandburg and Paul M. Angle, *Mary Lincoln: Wife and Widow* (New York: Harcourt & Co., 1932), 242.

Chapter

Disability
in the White House:
The Case of
Woodrow Wilson

John Milton Cooper, Jr.

Politically, American presidents can suffer a fate worse than death: disability. Fortunately — and perhaps verifying Otto von Bismarck's crack, "God protects fools, drunks, and the United States of America" — a severe disability has felled only two of the forty-two presidents since 1789. The first case seems to have made no historical waves. On July 2, 1881, an assassin shot and severely wounded James A. Garfield. The forty-nine-year-old president, who was just four months into his term, lingered in a conscious but bedridden condition for two and a half months until he died on September 19. He performed only one official act after he was shot — signing an extradition order — but no one tried to invoke Article II, section 1, of the Constitution, which states, "In case of [the president's] . . . inability to discharge the powers and duties of the said office, the same shall devolve on the Vice President." The country evidently fared tolerably well during that summer of 1881, and it is debatable whether Garfield's lingering demise constituted a true case of presidential disability.[1]

No similar luck or debate surrounds the other case. On October 2, 1919, Woodrow Wilson suffered a major stroke; about ten days later, he developed a prostate condition, which caused a urinary blockage with an attendant high fever that nearly killed him. For nearly a month after Wilson's stroke, almost no one saw the president except his wife, daughters, physician, and nurses. Only in November 1919 could he receive callers — mainly visiting royalty — and make one unpostponable major decision. The next two months, December 1919 and January 1920, witnessed some improvement and temporary setbacks in Wilson's condition. He saw a few more people, loosely superintended statements made in his name, and made occasional decisions. Still, during those two months he seldom left his bedroom, initiated next to no actions, composed almost no letters or speeches, and survived two bouts of influenza that brought him to the brink of resignation. Finally, in February 1920, Wilson recovered to a point at which he could manage a small measure of active participation in affairs of state, and he performed at that reduced level for his remaining year in office. Wilson, therefore, presents an incontrovertible case of presidential disability with demonstrable public consequences.[2]

This case turned the White House into something that it had been only once before and has, briefly, had to be only once again — an infirmary, convalescent facility, and hiding place for an incapacitated invalid. Garfield's disability had involved the presidential mansion in those roles for two months. While he stayed there, his doctors insisted on subjecting him to a rudimentary form of air-conditioning that weakened his constitution. Finally, they decided that he might stand a better chance of recovery away from Washington's notoriously oppressive summer climate, and the patient was transported to the seaside resort of Elberon, New Jersey. The doctors also insisted on repeatedly probing to remove the bullet from his abdomen, causing infections that likewise hastened his end. President Garfield owed his death, it seems, nearly as much to the good intentions of would-be healers as to the malice of a deranged assassin.[3]

Within a few years of Wilson's illness, the White House would serve as the domicile and hiding place for a man with a different sort of disability. Franklin Roosevelt's twelve-year tenancy, from March 1933 to April 1945, was the only time that a physically handicapped person has filled the office. Normal limitations on access to a president and special arrangements coalesced to abet the concealment of Roosevelt's inability to walk or stand without elaborate help. Guests at state dinners, for example, entered the State Dining Room to find the president already seated at the head table, and they would be ushered out and the doors closed before the staff brought in his wheelchair. On occasions when the president chose a standing position, the audience would enter one of the public rooms or the Rose Garden only after Roosevelt, wearing his steel braces, had taken his place behind a lectern. When he sometimes chose to "walk," he always traversed short distances leaning on such strong, experienced arms as those of his son James and his military aide, General Edwin "Pa" Watson. Visitors to the Oval Office grew so accustomed to Roosevelt's seated posture that in 1945 White House aides felt shocked when they saw President Truman get up and walk around.[4]

The concealment of Roosevelt's handicap extended far beyond the bounds of the White House. The press and a host of officials collaborated on innumerable occasions to stage scenes throughout the nation and abroad in what Hugh Gregory Gallagher has called "FDR's splendid deception." This situation was not comparable to Wilson's disability because no question was raised about Roosevelt's capacity to function as president. But such a question did arise with him during the last year and a half of his life, when he suffered from malignant, uncontrolled hypertension. The White House again served briefly as a hiding place, although Roosevelt spent much of his seclusion during 1944 at Bernard Baruch's South Carolina estate and elsewhere. Even at its worst, his hypertensive impairment did not compare with Wilson's disability. During these months, Roosevelt was able to travel extensively, including to the Yalta Conference, to run successfully for reelection, and to perform his duties most of the time.[5]

Both the nature of Wilson's disability and the response of his family and physicians contributed to its public consequences. Thanks to recently uncovered medical records, it is possible to say precisely what ailed Wilson. His doctor, Admiral Cary T. Grayson, had evidently suspected cerebrovascular trouble for about a week prior to the stroke. Grayson had accompanied Wilson in September 1919 on his speaking tour of middle-western and western states to urge American membership in the League of Nations. On that trip, Wilson had complained increasingly of blinding headaches and breathing difficulties; these were almost certainly symptoms of acute hypertension and congestive heart failure, often premonitory to a stroke or heart attack. After Wilson spoke at Pueblo, Colorado, on September 25, Grayson had noticed drooling and a drooping on the left side of his face. Those symptoms, together with the president's now-admitted exhaustion, impelled the doctor to order the remainder of the trip canceled in order to rush his patient back to Washington. Although Wilson seemed to recover with rest and seclusion in the White House, Grayson sent for Dr. Francis X. Dercum of Philadelphia, a leading neurologist who had treated Wilson off and on since 1906, to examine the president on October 3.[6]

The day before Dercum's visit, Wilson awoke with pronounced numbness in his left arm and leg. Mrs. Wilson later recalled helping him walk to the bathroom, where he allegedly fell, struck his head, and lost consciousness while she was telephoning Grayson. The physicians' contemporary reports, however, make no mention of a fall, saying only that the patient sank to the bedroom floor and did not lose consciousness. Upon seeing Wilson, Grayson immediately telephoned Dercum, who rushed to Washington and examined the president late in the afternoon of October 2, within a few hours of the stroke. His physical examination revealed "flaccid paralysis" in the left arm and leg and "hemiplegia" — loss of feeling — there and along the left side of the head, neck, and body. On the basis of his examination and Grayson's descriptions, the neurologist concluded that Wilson had suffered "a severe organic hemiplegia, probably due to a thrombosis of the middle cerebral artery of the right hemisphere." Dercum also ruled out what he called an "ingravescent hemorrhage," by which he meant the sudden attack, often followed by unconsciousness and death, that is usually conjured up by the word "stroke." In sum, Wilson's stroke was probably not life-threatening in itself, and the degree of permanent damage could not immediately be ascertained.[7]

Dercum examined Wilson three more times in October 1919, and an ophthalmologist examined the president once. Navy doctors and Mrs. Wilson's physician assisted Grayson in regular attendance, and when the prostate condition developed, a leading urologist, Hugh Young of the Johns Hopkins University School of Medicine, was summoned to examine the president and to advise about an operation to relieve the blockage. Young recommended against surgery, which would have been risky for a sixty-two-year-old man who had just suffered a stroke. Instead, drawing on his recent experience treating soldiers during World War I, Young predicted that, with continued application of hot compresses, the obstruction would clear by itself, as it did after four days. Dercum's subsequent examinations found that Wilson was regaining feeling in the stroke-affected areas, together with limited control over his left arm and leg. By December the president would be able to walk, haltingly, with a cane and to move his left arm a little. Throughout, all the physicians noted the patient's undiminished intellectual capacity, including his good-humored, often joking cooperation during their examinations.[8]

Those undiminished mental faculties presented the most misleading aspect of Wilson's condition. According to his wife's recollection, when Dr. Dercum gave her his diagnosis and prescribed rest for the president, she immediately asked, "Then had he better not resign, let Mr. Marshall [the vice president] succeed to the Presidency and let himself get that complete rest that is so vital to his life?" Dercum reportedly answered, "No. . . . For Mr. Wilson to resign would have a bad effect on the country, and a serious effect on our patient. He has staked his life and made his promise to the world to do all in his power to get the Treaty [of Versailles] ratified and make the League of Nations complete. If he resigns, the greatest incentive to recovery is gone; and as his mind is clear as crystal he can still do more with even a maimed body than anyone else." Strong grounds exist for doubting that the neurologist said those words in that way. Not only was Mrs. Wilson recalling their exchange after a lapse of nearly twenty years, but she also immediately vetoed full public disclosure of her husband's condition and subsequently spurned all suggestions of his relinquishing the presidency. It is more likely that Mrs. Wilson confused Dercum's and the other physicians' reassurances about the president's mental powers with their probable admission, almost surely prompted by her own questions, that remaining in office would supply a powerful incentive toward recovery.[9]

The way in which the president's wife grasped at the straw of his intellectual capacity would bring on a tragedy. The stroke most adversely affected Wilson's ability to perform his duties by diminishing his energy and altering his attitude. For nearly two months, Wilson lacked the physical energy needed to do even a minimal job in the White House. During the first month after the stroke, he never left his bed, even to go to the bathroom. Thereafter, he could sit up, and he began to be wheeled around in an Atlantic City boardwalk chair, at first indoors and later on short airings outside. Wilson did not leave the White House grounds until March 1920, when he took his first automobile ride in five months. During those months he passed most of his waking hours in silence, broken by brief conversations with his wife, his daughter Margaret, and Grayson. Because he suffered from double vision after the stroke, reading seemed beyond him, and Mrs. Wilson and Margaret found that at first he could listen to them read aloud to him only for brief periods. The few occasions on which Wilson received visitors required elaborate preparations and carefully staged encounters and left him exhausted. By any reasonable measure, the United States did not have a functioning president between the beginning of October 1919 and the end of January 1920.

Bad as the depletion of Wilson's energy was, the impact of the stroke on his psychological makeup was even worse. Both during the initial period of near-total debilitation and, more pronouncedly, after his partial recovery in February, his personality displayed what present-day neurologists term a "focal psychosyndrome." In such cases, the patient loses much of his or her control over emotions and capacity for judgment, while certain basic personality traits become so exaggerated as to create, in the words of the neurologist Dr. Bert E. Park, "a caricature of himself." In Wilson, tenacity and self-reliance metamorphosed into stubbornness and self-righteousness. Another effect of this syndrome is severe impairment in the ability to adapt to changes in circumstances and to deal with current realities. Wilson gave the clearest evidence of all these effects in his repeated failure to deal constructively with the Senate struggle over whether to attach reservations on American membership in the League of Nations to its consent to the Treaty of Versailles. At two critical junctures, the president rejected a growing and, finally, near-unanimous chorus of entreaties to compromise. In the first instance, he croaked defiance from his sickbed at his adversaries and

President Wilson and his wife Edith, who controlled access to the chief executive during his severe, prolonged illness. Harris & Ewing.

critics; in the second, he worked somewhat actively to scuttle biparti-san efforts at reconciliation.[10]

To complicate matters further, almost no one outside the president's inner circle of family and physicians knew the true nature of his condi-tion. There is no evidence that Wilson himself was told or consulted about the nature of his illness, and it is questionable that he ever admit-ted to himself that he had suffered a stroke. From the beginning, and apparently against Grayson's and the other doctors' advice, Mrs. Wilson embargoed any disclosure of her husband's stroke. Dr. Grayson repeat-edly told the press that Wilson suffered from "nervous exhaustion," was responding well to treatment, and would achieve "complete recovery." Everyone involved acted with the best of intentions. Edith Bolling Galt Wilson was fiercely determined to see the man she loved and admired get well, and she seems to have weighed his presidential responsibilities almost entirely from the standpoint of their therapeutic value for him. Understandably, therefore, she recoiled from the likely inferences that other people, particularly Wilson's political foes, might draw from the news that he had suffered a stroke. As physicians, Grayson and his as-sociates felt bound by their obligation to respect the wishes of their patient as expressed by his next of kin. Moreover, in view of the uncer-tain extent of the stroke's effects, public reticence about the condition seemed warranted.[11]

Still, no matter how benignly motivated, this policy amounted to a cover-up that deprived the public of vital information. Full disclosure might have prompted demands for Wilson's resignation and might, as feared, have hurt his chances for recovery. As matters transpired, how-ever, the political fallout from nondisclosure helped to destroy what remained of his presidency. This cover-up succeeded no better than most others have done in Washington. Grayson's relentlessly optimistic statements flew in the face of the plain facts of Wilson's failure to be seen in public, to give speeches, or to show signs of real leadership. Ru-mors periodically cropped up about his having died or gone mad. Bars that had been put up before the turn of the century now became "proof" that the White House was harboring a lunatic. Knowledge about the stroke could not be contained, either. Some cabinet members found out about it right away, and accounts gradually percolated through the medical community. Within two weeks of the stroke, public allegations surfaced when reporters picked up a Republican senator's statement to a constituent. Grayson artfully denied the allegation without saying that the president had not suffered a stroke. Finally, in February 1920, one of the president's physicians, Dr. Young, the urologist, stated in an interview praising Wilson's progress in rehabilitation that he had suffered "a cerebral thrombosis." Once more, Grayson, joined by the other attending physicians, castigated the report's propriety without actually denying its validity.[12]

This flap among the medical men could not have come at a worse time for the president's political standing. Besides intransigence on the League issue, Wilson showed other signs of rigidity and apparent petulance in his newfound relative activism. Another sign came when he publicly rejected any accommodation toward Italy's territorial claims along the Adriatic coast and threatened to withdraw from the whole peace settlement. Worse still, Wilson forced Secretary of State Robert Lansing to resign on the pretext of having convened unconstitutional cabinet meetings during the president's illness. These events, particularly Lansing's dismissal, unleashed a wave of condemnation from the press. Up to this time, editorial opinion had tended to combine impatience at domestic problems and the deadlock over the peace treaty with some slowness to blame the president. Now, however, leading newspapers made such declarations as this: "If his judgment in the Lansing case be a specimen of the fully restored mental vigor of which Dr. Young has lately assured us, the country is indeed in sore straits." Those reactions and the dismay that greeted final defeat of the treaty in March 1920 pushed Wilson's administration and his party down the slide toward massive repudiation in the polls the following November. Warren Harding's "normalcy," twelve years of probusiness Republican conservatism, and nearly two decades of retreat from international commitment were all just around the corner.[13]

But Americans did not have to wait months or years to suffer the consequences of Wilson's disability. What happened during the six months following his stroke more than sufficed to sow misery. Big strikes occurred in the coal and steel industries late in 1919 and early in 1920. In the case of the coal strike, pleas for presidential intervention brought no response from the White House, because Wilson was too enervated to act. Soon afterward, Attorney General A. Mitchell Palmer pounced upon rampant antiradical sentiment as he rounded up resident aliens for deportation and raided offices of left-wing organizations and homes of leftist leaders to seize files and conduct mass arrests. The president evidently knew nothing about this "Red Scare" and his own cabinet officer's part in it.

The government continued to function, thanks mainly to well-established routines and to Wilson's collegial style of management, which allowed cabinet officers great latitude in running their departments. The exception to that style had been in foreign affairs, where the president's dominance, together with his long-standing disdain for Lansing, lodged most major decisions in his hands. The secretary of state tried to cope as well as he could, but his almost daily pleas to Mrs. Wilson to have the president advise him about critical negotiations and unfilled diplomatic appointments went unanswered. Major domestic posts also stayed vacant for months, and of the three cabinet changes that occurred between November 1919 and March 1920, the only one that resulted in a first-rate replacement came when David F. Houston agreed to shift from the Agriculture Department to the Treasury. The pressing domestic issue of returning the nation's railroads and telegraph lines to private management after wartime control got handled by default, mainly by the president's secretary and the director-general of the railroads, because Wilson's attention could not be engaged more than sporadically and momentarily. The word most commonly used to describe affairs of state at the end of 1919 and the beginning of 1920 was "mess."[14]

Blame for these and other sins of omission did not fall solely on Wilson. The arrangements devised to facilitate his recovery practically guaranteed neglect of affairs of state. Responsibility for those arrangements belonged to his wife and doctors. As Mrs. Wilson recalled, Dercum instructed her, "Have everything come to you; weigh the importance of each matter, and see if it is possible by consultation with the respective heads of the Departments to solve them without the guidance of your husband. But always keep in mind that every time you take him a new anxiety, problem to excite him, you are turning a knife in an open wound." Once more, it is doubtful that the neurologist or any other physician offered such categorical advice about how to run the government. Nor was the passivity that Mrs. Wilson retrospectively imputed to herself at all in character for that strong-willed woman. It is more likely that Edith Wilson devised the arrangements herself after rejecting the option of resignation and questioning the physicians about how to give her husband the rest they prescribed.[15]

Making such arrangements opened Mrs. Wilson to charges of usurpation. Rumors about "government by petticoat" soon filled the vacuum of information about the president's condition, and scholars later criticized her for overstepping herself by controlling access of people and information to her husband. In fact, Mrs. Wilson tried scrupulously to avoid infringing on policy matters, and at least some of the material that she withheld had no business on the president's desk, anyway. Furthermore, if Edith Wilson had attempted to act as Wilson's surrogate, she would have been well qualified to do so, since he had made her his closest political confidante and shared secrets of state with her even before their marriage in 1915.[16]

Slightly weightier charges of usurpation might be leveled against Wilson's secretary, Joseph P. Tumulty. An affable, politically astute Irish-American, Joe Tumulty had served for almost nine years as Wilson's secretary, since the latter's election as governor of New Jersey. Even when he was in the best of health, Wilson had relied on Tumulty both as a domestic political intelligence gatherer who surveyed newspaper opinion and picked up gossip, and as a lobbyist who performed the endless small acts of attention, persuasion, and flattery that the chief executive himself found distasteful. As a result, Tumulty had to fill much of the void left by Wilson's isolation. Although he never acted against the president's wishes, in at least one instance, the veto of the prohibition-enforcing Volstead Act, the secretary almost certainly spoke in his chief's name without his knowledge. Tumulty also assumed a function that neither he nor anyone else had ever performed for Wilson before, that of ghostwriter. The state of the union message to Congress in December 1919 was his work, only cursorily reviewed by the president. A month later, the call to the Democratic party to make the next election a "great and solemn referendum" on the League of Nations also came in Tumulty's words, although by now Wilson could listen to and revise drafts of the statement. Such as they were, Tumulty's assumptions of the presidential mantle were few and limited, and he had to fly solo most of the time, since he was not allowed to see the president at all until mid-November.[17]

Without question, the omissions that flowed from Wilson's disability and the ways that those closest to him handled the situation gravely wounded the American body politic. But those wounds by neglect were not the worst of it. The one piece of public business that did reach the president following his stroke occasioned the most momentous harm of all — to his country and, in all likelihood, to the world. This was the conflict over American membership in the League of Nations. Wilson's stroke occurred at an especially critical juncture in what was being called the "League fight." During the summer of 1919, he had dickered with various senators over reservations that might define or limit American participation in the League. Although Wilson publicly resisted any reservations, he privately drafted a set of interpretations that could accompany but not be part of the instrument of ratification of the treaty, and he gave those interpretative reservations to the leader of the Democratic minority in the Senate, Gilbert M. Hitchcock of Nebraska. Meanwhile, the majority leader, Henry Cabot Lodge of Massachusetts, who was also chairman of the Foreign Relations Committee, lined up most of his fellow Republicans on the committee and in the Senate behind a set of much more strictly limiting reservations, which were to be incorporated into the instrument of ratification.[18]

Whether Wilson should have left Washington to make his speaking tour in September 1919 or kept negotiating with a small swing group of "mild reservationist" Republican senators remains a matter of dispute among historians. Indisputably, however, the time for hard bargaining and delicate diplomacy across party lines had arrived by early October, just when the stroke felled Wilson. His removal from the scene deprived his side of effective representation in the pulling and hauling that resulted in adoption of Lodge's reservations by a Senate majority. When consent to the treaty first came to a vote, therefore, on November 19, 1919, League supporters faced the unappetizing choice between membership limited by the Lodge reservations or staying out.[19]

At this point, Wilson compounded the damage already done by his nonparticipation with an all-or-nothing approach. The League situation in the Senate was the one piece of public business that Mrs. Wilson had not kept from her husband except during the medical crisis of his urinary blockage. Sometime around October 20, less than three weeks after the president's stroke, she allowed Senator Hitchcock to see him briefly. Hitchcock was Wilson's first visitor from beyond the inner circle, before any cabinet members, royal callers, or even Tumulty. The senator saw Wilson twice more before the vote, and he wrote almost daily reports on the situation to Mrs. Wilson, who read or summarized them for the president. In all those meetings and communications, Wilson insisted that the Lodge reservations were totally unacceptable; he refused to contemplate any alternatives; he would not divulge his authorship of the interpretative reservations; and he demanded votes against consent with reservations attached to the instrument of ratification.[20]

All but three Democratic senators bowed to the president's wishes and joined with the dozen or so "irreconcilables" who opposed League membership under any conditions to defeat consent to the treaty, forty-one ayes to fifty nays. Lodge then permitted a vote on consent without reservations, and all the Republicans except one mild reservationist joined the irreconcilables to block consent again, thirty-eight ayes to fifty-three nays. This deadlock, which left the United States outside the League and officially still at war, would not have occurred if Wilson had not played his stroke-induced roles, first of forced inaction and then of unrealistic intransigence. Outside a small isolationist minority, public opinion greeted the treaty's twin defeats with dismay. Few commentators blamed the president exclusively, however, both because he had made a powerful case for his position on his speaking tour and because Lodge had failed even more conspicuously than Wilson to present himself in an attractive or conciliatory light. Interestingly, too, leading Democratic senators did not seem upset over the outcome. They expected these votes to clear the air and bring public pressure for compromise to bear on the Republicans. They predicted correctly. When Congress reconvened in December, the mild reservationists got busy exploring common ground with the Democrats, and bipartisan talks with Lodge opened in January 1920. Here, at long last, was the kind of serious effort at compromise that should have occurred earlier and almost certainly would have if a healthy, clear-headed Wilson had been on the scene.[21]

As matters transpired, these compromise efforts nearly did lead to a happier, more constructive ending of the League fight. Once more, however, the hand that threw the monkey wrench belonged to Wilson. On December 14, 1919, the stricken president made two moves. One was to walk for the first time, taking a few steps around his bedroom. The other was to issue a statement, apparently dictated by him, asserting, "He [the president] has no compromise or concession of any kind in mind, but intends, so far as he is concerned, that the Republican leaders of the Senate shall continue to bear the undivided responsibility for the fate of the treaty and the present condition of the world in consequence of that fate." During the next three months, Wilson never budged from that obdurate stand. Instead, he tried to attack his adversaries. Also, in his short-lived flush of energy in mid-December, he had a letter drafted, probably by Tumulty, in which he called on fifty-six senators — even some supporters, as well as opponents and critics — to resign their seats and face special elections on the League issue; if enough Republicans won, he said he would appoint a Republican secretary of state, and he and the vice president would then resign and make that Republican president at once. Although this scheme never saw the light of day, Wilson did have his wife request information from the attorney general about various states' provisions for filling senatorial vacancies. The idea formed the basis for his "great and solemn referendum" message to the Democrats in January 1920.[22]

To his credit, Tumulty tried for a while to nudge his chief toward compromise. Early in January, he urged Wilson to announce his support for interpretative reservations, and he enlisted the aid of Secretary of the Treasury Houston in inserting several sentences to that effect into the otherwise defiant message to the Democrats. Working closely with Hitchcock and Lansing, Tumulty cooperated with the bipartisan negotiations in the Senate. At one point, Tumulty drafted a detailed statement on reservations, but Wilson came down with some kind of flu around January 21, and when he recovered, he eliminated most of the specifics and the conciliatory language. Meanwhile, under pressure from irreconcilables who threatened to bolt the Republican party, Lodge had withdrawn from the bipartisan talks.[23]

Then, at the beginning of February, Wilson suffered another flu-like illness that evidently brought him to the verge of resignation. What transpired at this juncture is not completely clear from surviving records. Grayson later wrote a memorandum to himself, "Look up notes re President Wilson's intention to go to the Senate in a wheeled chair for the purpose of resigning." In September 1920 the doctor also talked to John W. Davis, the ambassador to Great Britain, about "advice given to Pres[ident] last January to resign, his [Grayson's] inclination, & Mrs. W[ilson]'s persuasion to the contrary." About three months later, Grayson told Ray Stannard Baker, the journalist and former press secretary at the peace conference, that Wilson "talked with Grayson about resigning last January. Grayson advised it strongly on health grounds. But Mrs. W[ilson] objected." Earlier, on February 4, the president had sent word to Baker "that he 'might have a message' for me. There is something 'on.' " Arthur S. Link, the editor of *The Papers of Woodrow Wilson*, and his associates have speculated that the recurrent bouts of flu may have made Wilson despair of coping with the demands of his office. They also believe that what tipped the balance against resignation, even more than Mrs. Wilson's resistance, was the "euphoria" that he soon felt over his partial recovery, together with his simultaneous indignation when the former British foreign secretary, Viscount Grey of Fallodon, publicly suggested that the European Allies might accept American ratification of the peace treaty with the Lodge reservations.[24]

Those efforts at compromise and resignation in January and early February marked the nearest approach to a different outcome to the League fight. Although Mrs. Wilson resisted the attempt to get her husband to resign, she joined in the campaign for compromise. When Baker talked with her on January 22, he "found her in full accord" with his own ideas about the president mounting an initiative toward conciliation. But Mrs. Wilson also revealed how badly the stroke had warped her husband's judgment and how little real chance existed for compromise. When Baker argued that the fate of the League was hanging in the balance, she responded, "I know but the President has in mind the reception he got in the west, and he believes the people are with him." Baker grasped the point at once. "That is the trouble," he wrote in his diary. "He has been ill since last October & he cannot know what is going on." Both Mrs. Wilson and Grayson told Baker that they could not move the president. Whenever they mentioned compromise, Baker noted, "He hardens at any such suggestion: the very moment of yielding anything to the Senate seems to drive him into stubborn immovability."[25]

Regrettably, Wilson's recovery from the second illness and his new-found energy in February 1920 worsened the situation. Determined to take charge, the president not only forced Lansing out and threatened to withdraw from the peace settlement over the Adriatic dispute, but also issued a stinging rebuke to Grey's suggestion and proceeded to stifle one last stab at a compromise in the Senate. When Carter Glass, who had just left the cabinet to fill a Senate vacancy from Virginia, proposed a middle-ground position on the most important reservation, Wilson dictated a reply restating his view "that absolute inaction on our part is better than a mistaken initiative." At this juncture, Tumulty, who had been out of his depth in handling matters of high policy, reverted to his accustomed roles of uncritical subordinate and political operator as he lobbied energetically to stop a stampede of Democratic senators toward consent with the Lodge reservations.[26]

The secretary also continued in his new capacity of ghostwriter by drafting most of Wilson's letter to Hitchcock on March 8, 1920, which dashed the last frail hopes of compromise. In a final fatal pronouncement supplied by Tumulty, Wilson avowed, "I have been struck by the fact that practically every so-called reservation was in effect a rather sweeping nullification of the terms of the treaty itself. I hear of reservationists and mild reservationists, but I cannot understand the difference between a nullifier and a mild nullifier." Those words sufficed to quell much of the senatorial revolt. On March 19, 1920, four months to the day after the first votes, the Senate again failed to consent to the Treaty of Versailles with the Lodge reservations. This time, however, forty-nine senators, a majority that included twenty-one Democrats, voted in favor, while twenty-three other Democrats and a dozen Republican irreconcilables voted against. A switch of seven votes would have supplied the two-thirds required for consent. More than enough Democrats would have gone over if the president had merely held his peace.[27]

It is important to be clear about what was at stake in this second, final defeat of the treaty. A two-thirds vote for consent with the Lodge reservations would not have ended the League fight. Wilson had repeatedly pledged to withhold ratification — the equivalent to a presidential veto in the treaty-making process — if the Senate acted on any terms except his own. But consent blocked by presidential action would have changed the political complexion of the debate by giving the Republicans a stake in joining the League on their terms. Instead, Lodge himself now blocked all attempts to commit the party to membership with his reservations, and he engineered the straddle in the Republicans' 1920 platform and campaign, which condemned "Wilson's League" and advocated an unspecified "association of nations." Despite efforts by pro-League Republicans, the election did become a referendum on the issue, in which the Republicans' staggering landslide could only be read as some degree of repudiation. The incoming Harding administration soon followed the path of least resistance by abandoning both League membership and any effort at forming an alternative international organization.[28]

Wilson had often declared that America's refusal to join the League of Nations would "break the heart of the world," and, indeed, the outcome was tragic. That is not to say, as many maintained then and later, that the failure to work out a compromise would lead inexorably to another global conflict. Only the kind of wholehearted, lasting commitment to the peace settlement and collective security that Wilson advocated would have prevented the international breakdown that began a decade later. By those lights, the president did right to hold out against the limits that his adversaries wanted to set on American participation in a new world order. But his disability led him into tragic error when he refused to recognize that even limited formal participation in that order would have constructively altered the context of the nation's foreign policy. Such later moves as undercutting League efforts to resist Japanese aggression in Manchuria in 1931 and 1932 and the wholesale embrace of isolationism soon afterward would have become less likely. Such a changed context of American foreign policy might not have prevented the deterioration of international order that culminated in World

War II, but it is difficult to imagine a less promising outcome than what happened in 1919 and 1920.

Taken together, the sins of omission and commission that can be traced to Wilson's disability caused the worst breakdown of American government except for the Civil War. Furthermore, nothing except Wilson's voluntary resignation could have avoided the breakdown. The vagueness of Article II, section 1, effectively ruled out any alternative. Vice President Thomas R. Marshall made himself close to invisible during these months, and the only high-ranking official in the executive branch to suggest replacing the president was Secretary of State Lansing. At a cabinet meeting on October 6, Lansing recommended calling on the vice president to take over, but, according to the diary of the secretary of the navy, others immediately raised questions about "what constitutes inability & who is to decide it." Someone then requested that Grayson be summoned to the meeting. When the doctor arrived, Lansing questioned him about the nature and duration of the president's illness and the clarity of his mind. "My reply," Grayson recorded immediately afterward, "was that the President's mind was not only clear but very active, and that he clearly showed that he was very much annoyed when he found that the Cabinet had been called and that he wanted to know by whose authority the meeting had been called and for what purpose."[29]

The only other feeler toward the possibility of removing Wilson originated on Capitol Hill. As soon as Congress reconvened at the beginning of December 1919, talk arose about the president's condition, and the Republican majority on the Senate Foreign Relations Committee used the pretext of diplomatic troubles with Mexico to have two members request a visit with the president. This senatorial mission, waggishly dubbed the "smelling committee," consisted of Hitchcock and Albert Fall of New Mexico, a Republican irreconcilable. Grayson surprised them by granting immediate access, and they visited Wilson for forty minutes on the afternoon of December 5. The president, who lay in bed with his impaired left side covered, knowledgeably discussed Mexican affairs, picked up papers from the bedside table with his right hand, and joked about politics and his health. Both senators immediately told reporters that they had found the president alert and attentive, while Fall declared, "In my opinion, Mr. Wilson is perfectly capable of handling the situation. He seemed to me in excellent trim, both mentally and physically, for a man who has been in bed for ten weeks." According to the *New York Times*, Fall and Hitchcock's account silenced "the many wild and often unfriendly rumors of Presidential disability."[30]

Those incidents demonstrated the impossibility of removing Wilson without his consent. The critical consideration was less a matter of who could certify "inability" than the meaning of the term. So long as the president's intellectual capacity was unimpaired, and so long as genuine hope for recovery existed, what physician could unequivocally pronounce him unable to fill his office? The deeper aspect of Wilson's incapacity lay in his impaired judgment and other psychological deformations, which were beyond the ken of any medical specialists in 1919. This case of presidential disability left the United States in a box with no way out.

In the end, the question has to be asked, could it happen again? Could this country suffer a comparably disastrous case of presidential disability? The answer is yes. The only mitigating factor today may be the far greater intrusiveness of the mass media, particularly the television-spawned appetite for the sights and sounds of a president. Probably no occupant of the White House can ever again enjoy as much seclusion as Wilson did, or as much concealment as Franklin Roosevelt. Still, it would be imprudent to underestimate future ingenuity in attempting such cover-ups. The Twenty-fifth Amendment to the Constitution affords much less protection than is commonly believed. Section 4 of this amendment requires that the vice president "and a majority of either the principal officers of the executive departments or of such other body as Congress may by law provide" must declare the president "unable to discharge the powers and duties of his office." This provision seems to require nothing short of a coup d'état to be imposed on a nonconsenting chief executive, particularly because this section further stipulates that when the president declares "that no inability exists, he shall resume the powers and duties of his office" unless the vice president and the majority of the cabinet or congressionally sanctioned body decide otherwise. Imagine anyone trying to exercise those options with Wilson in 1919.[31]

The deepest danger of presidential disability revealed in Wilson's case lies beyond any readily demonstrable physical incapacity. This president's disability caused its greatest harm through his skewed emotions and warped judgment. Unless psychiatry becomes a much more solidly scientific and universally accepted branch of medicine, it seems questionable whether any real protection can be raised against these aspects of presidential disability. The inescapability of its consequences is what makes Wilson's case, and the potential for others like it, truly tragic. At one point in January 1920, he said to Grayson, "It would probably have been better if I had died last fall." Woodrow Wilson was right. For him, his country, and the world, disability was a fate worse than death. Bismarck's dictum notwithstanding, there is no guarantee against such a fate again befalling the United States of America.[32]

NOTES

1. On Garfield's last months, see Allan Poskin, *Garfield* (Kent, Ohio: Kent State University Press, 1978), 594–608, and Justus D. Doenecke, *The Presidencies of James A. Garfield and Chester A. Arthur* (Lawrence: University Press of Kansas, 1981), 53–54. In addition to accounts of disability, there is a growing literature on presidential illness. For treatments of the twentieth-century ones, see Bert Edward Park, *The Impact of Illness on World Leaders* (Philadelphia: University of Pennsylvania Press, 1986), chaps. 1 and 4; Kenneth R. Crispell and Carlos F. Gomez, *Hidden Illness in the White House* (Durham, N.C.: Duke University Press, 1988); Robert H. Ferrell, *Ill-Advised: Presidential Health and Public Trust* (Columbia: University of Missouri Press, 1992), and Robert E. Gilbert, *The Mortal Presidency: Illness and Anguish in the White House* (New York: Basic Books, 1992). By far the best treatment of Wilson's illness, however, is the as yet unpublished essay by Bert E. Park and Arthur S. Link, "Woodrow Wilson's Fate, 1919–1920" (1992, in authors' possession).

2. For the two most recent treatments of the last days of the Wilson presidency, see August Heckscher, *Woodrow Wilson: A Biography* (New York: Charles Scribner's Sons, 1991), 611–44, and Kendrick A. Clements, *The Presidency of Woodrow Wilson* (Lawrence: University Press of Kansas, 1992), 197–224.

3. On Garfield's assassin, see Charles Rosenberg, *The Trial of Assassin Guiteau: Psychiatry and Law in the Gilded Age* (Chicago: University of Chicago Press, 1968).

4. The best treatment of Roosevelt's concealment of his handicap is in Hugh Gregory Gallagher, *FDR's Splendid Deception* (New York: Dodd, Mead & Co.,

1985). For the shock at seeing a standing, walking president, see David Mc-Cullough, *Truman* (New York: Simon & Schuster, 1992), 364. One source for this observation is George M. Elsey, then a naval aide in the White House and most recently a member of the planning committee for the White House bicentennial symposium.

5. On Roosevelt's hypertension, see Park, *Impact of Illness on World Leaders*, 221–94; Crispell and Gomez, *Hidden Illness in the White House*, 75–120; Ferrell, *Ill-Advised*, 28–48, and Gilbert, *Mortal Presidency*, 48–73.

6. Cary T. Grayson memorandum, n.d., in *The Papers of Woodrow Wilson*, ed. Arthur S. Link, 67 vols. (Princeton, N.J.: Princeton University Press, 1966–92), 64: 507–10. The *Wilson Papers* editors believe that this memorandum was written sometime in late 1919 or early 1920, probably to prepare for a possible congressional investigation of Wilson's condition, ibid., 507 n. 1. For accounts of the recovery of Grayson's medical papers, see ibid., ix, and *Princeton Alumni Weekly* (January 23, 1991).

7. Grayson memorandum, *Wilson Papers* 64: 507–8; Dercum memorandum, October 20, 1919, ibid., 500–502. For the story of Wilson's fall, see Irwin Hood Hoover memoir, n.d., ibid. 63: 633–34; Hoover, *Forty-Two Years at the White House* (Boston: Houghton Mifflin Co., 1934), 100–102, and Edith Bolling Galt Wilson, *My Memoir* (Indianapolis: Bobbs-Merrill Co., 1939), 287–88. For recent examinations of Grayson's and Dercum's reports by neurologists, see James F. Toole to Arthur S. Link, June 12, 1990, *Wilson Papers* 64: 505–6 n. 11, and Bert E. Park to Link, [June 1990], ibid., 506–7 n. 11. For two other retrospective diagnoses of Wilson's stroke made by neurologists before these reports were uncovered, see Park, "Woodrow Wilson's Stroke of October 2, 1919," ibid. 63: 639–46, and Edwin A. Weinstein, *Woodrow Wilson: A Medical and Psychological Biography* (Princeton, N.J.: Princeton University Press, 1988), 357. Weinstein lays special stress on the likelihood of a preexisting history of carotid artery occlusion; see ibid., 165–66, 252.

8. On Young's treatment, see *New York Times*, October 18, 1919, and *Wilson Papers* 63: 578 n. 1. For Dercum's subsequent examinations, see Dercum memorandum, October 20, 1919, ibid. 64: 502–5, and Grayson memorandum, ibid., 508–10.

9. E. Wilson, *My Memoir*, 289. Dercum's and Grayson's memoranda do not mention their giving Mrs. Wilson advice about the question of resignation. Mrs. Wilson wrote *My Memoir* over the space of eleven years, completing the book in October 1938, and this passage comes in the last part.

10. Park, "The Aftermath of Wilson's Stroke," *Wilson Papers* 64: 525–28. Cf. Weinstein, *Wilson*, 358–60.

11. Grayson's statements to the press are published in *Wilson Papers* 63 and 64. In fairness to Mrs. Wilson's judgment, it should be noted that there was political shrewdness of a sort in concealing the nature and extent of the presi-

dent's illness from the public, in view of prevailing public beliefs that serious illnesses or handicaps disqualified people from political leadership or any kind of active life. An instructive comparison comes from the lengths to which Franklin Roosevelt went less than ten years later to conceal and minimize public awareness of his inability to walk. On those public attitudes and FDR's cover-up, see Gallagher, *FDR's Splendid Deception*, esp. 28–33, and Geoffrey C. Ward, *A First-Class Temperament: The Emergence of Franklin Roosevelt* (New York: Harper & Row, 1989), esp. 618–20.

12. Secretary of State Robert Lansing evidently suspected a stroke immediately from the way the president's secretary, Joseph P. Tumulty, gestured toward his left side when he first told him of the illness. See Robert Lansing, desk diary, October 3, [1919], *Wilson Papers* 63: 547. In February 1920, a prominent Chicago physician asserted, "It soon became fairly widely known, in spite of every effort at secrecy, that the President had suffered a stroke, with resulting paralysis of one arm and leg." Dr. Arthur Dean Bevan in *Philadelphia Press*, February 16, 1920, ibid. 64: 431. By that time, the urologist, Dr. Young, had already stated that Wilson had suffered a stroke. *New York Times*, February 11, 1920. The first public allegation of a stroke came from Senator George H. Moses, a Republican from New Hampshire. See ibid., October 12, 1919. For Grayson's artful non-denial, see ibid., October 13, 1919.

13. For press reactions, see *Literary Digest* 64 (February 28, 1920), 13–15. The newspaper quoted is the *New York Globe*, which was politically independent in affiliation.

14. For accounts of these events, see Robert K. Murray, *Red Scare: A Study in National Hysteria, 1919 and 1920* (Minneapolis: University of Minnesota Press, 1955); Stanley Coben, *A. Mitchell Palmer: Politician* (New York: Columbia University Press, 1963), 212–45, and Bill Noggle, *Into the Twenties: The United States from the Armistice to Normalcy* (Urbana: University of Illinois Press, 1974), 84–121.

15. E. Wilson, *My Memoir*, 289. This judgment about Dercum's and the other physicians' reticence in suggesting to Mrs. Wilson how to run the White House concurs with Weinstein, *Wilson*, 360, which notes that Dercum was dead by the time her book was published, as was Grayson.

16. For Mrs. Wilson's own account of the workings of the White House under her "stewardship," see *My Memoir*, 289–97.

17. On the Volstead Act, see veto message, October 27, 1919, *Wilson Papers* 63: 601, and for the assertion that Tumulty acted without Wilson's knowledge, see ibid., 602 n. 1, 638 n. 6. On the state of the union message, see Tumulty to Edith Wilson, [November 24, 1919], ibid. 64: 72, with enclosed draft, ibid., 73–87, and I. H. Hoover memoir, ibid. 63: 638. For the "great and solemn referendum" message, see Tumulty draft, [January 6, 1920], ibid. 64: 247–49, and David F. Houston, *Eight Years with Wilson's Cabinet*, 2 vols. (Garden City, N.Y.: Dou-

bleday, Page & Co., 1926), 2: 47–48. On Tumulty's role, see also John M. Blum, *Joe Tumulty and the Wilson Era* (Boston: Houghton Mifflin Co., 1951), 230–39.

18. The interpretative reservations are in a Wilson memorandum, [September 3, 1919], *Wilson Papers* 62: 621. See also Gilbert M. Hitchcock to Edith Wilson, January 5, 1920, ibid. 64: 244. On Lodge's position, see Henry Cabot Lodge, *The Senate and the League of Nations* (New York: Charles Scribner's Sons, 1925), chaps. 9, 10; John A. Garraty, *Henry Cabot Lodge: A Biography* (New York: Alfred A. Knopf, 1953), 365–78, and William C. Widenor, *Henry Cabot Lodge and the Search for an American Foreign Policy* (Berkeley: University of California Press, 1980), 328–48.

19. On the tour, see John Milton Cooper, Jr., "Fool's Errand or Finest Hour? Woodrow Wilson's Speaking Tour, September, 1919," in *The Wilson Era: Essays in Honor of Arthur S. Link,* ed. John Milton Cooper and Charles E. Neu (Arlington Heights, Ill.: Harlan Davidson, 1991), 198–220.

20. On Hitchcock's meetings with Wilson, see *Wilson Papers* 64: 45 n. 1; Lansing to Edith Wilson, January 12, 1920, ibid., 272; Lansing desk diary, January 13, 1920, ibid., 274; Grayson memorandum, November 17, 1919, ibid., 43–45; *New York Times,* November 18, 1919. For their communications, see Hitchcock to Edith Wilson, November 13, 15, 17, 1919, *Wilson Papers* 64: 28–29, 37–38, 50–51; Wilson to Hitchcock (drafted by Hitchcock), November 18, 1919, ibid., 58.

21. For the votes, see *Congressional Record,* 66th Congress, 1st Session, 8800, 8803 (November 19, 1919). For the Democratic senators' reactions, see Oscar W. Underwood to Wilson, November 21, 1919, *Wilson Papers* 64: 69–70; Hitchcock to Wilson, November 22, 1919, ibid., 70; *New York Times,* November 25, 1919.

22. *New York Times,* December 15, 1919. For the senatorial and/or presidential resignation scheme, see Wilson draft letter, [ca. December 17, 1919], *Wilson Papers* 64: 199–202; Edith Wilson to A. Mitchell Palmer, December 18, 1919, ibid., 202–3; Palmer to E. Wilson, ibid., 214–15. The part of the scheme that called for his own resignation and replacement by a Republican previously appointed secretary of state recalled Wilson's secret plan in 1916 to vacate the presidency in favor of his opponent Charles Evans Hughes in the event of Wilson's losing the election. See Arthur S. Link, *Wilson: Campaigns of Progressivism and Peace, 1916–1917* (Princeton, N.J.: Princeton University Press, 1965), 153–56.

23. For Tumulty's efforts, see Lansing desk diary, January 13, 14, 15, 1920, *Wilson Papers* 64: 274, 276, 282; Tumulty to Edith Wilson, January 15, 16, 17, 1920, ibid., 276–77, 282–83, 287; Tumulty draft letter, January 15, 1920, ibid., 278–82. See also ibid., 277 n. 1, 278 n. 1, 287 n. 1. On the compromise negotiations, see Hitchcock to Tumulty, January 16, 17, 1920, ibid., 283–84, 288–95; Hitchcock to Wilson, January 22, 1920, ibid., 312; *New York Times,* January 23, 24, 1920. See also the observations of the editors, *Wilson Papers* 64: 328 n. 2.

Lodge is totally silent about these negotiations in his own correspondence in the Henry Cabot Lodge Papers, Massachusetts Historical Society.

24. Grayson memorandum, n.d., quoted in *Wilson Papers* 64: 361 n. 1; John W. Davis diary, September 2, 1920, quoted in ibid.; Ray Stannard Baker diary, November 28, 1920, quoted in ibid.; Baker diary, February 4, 1920, ibid., 362. See also observations of editors, ibid., 363 n. 1. According to Grayson, Wilson again discussed resignation in April, but the account makes the president's comments sound as if they reflected less a settled plan than a mood of temporary discouragement, coupled with bitterness at erstwhile supporters, particularly Colonel Edward M. House. See Grayson memorandum, April 13, 1920, ibid. 65: 179–80.

25. Baker diary, January 23, 1920, ibid. 64: 320–21.

26. Wilson to Carter Glass (E. Wilson draft), [February 11, 1920], ibid., 405. See also Glass to Wilson, February 9, 12, 1920, ibid., 387–88, 410–11; Tumulty to E. Wilson, March 1, 1920, ibid. 65: 24–25.

27. Wilson to Hitchcock, drafts, [ca. February 28], March 1, 5, 1920, ibid. 65: 7–9, 11–14, 25–28, 30–35, 49–55. That sentence first appeared in the last draft, ibid., 54. The letter was finally sent as Wilson to Hitchcock, March 8, 1920, ibid., 67–71. For the vote, see *Congressional Record*, 66th Congress, 2nd Session, 4599 (March 19, 1920).

28. On Lodge's later role, see Garraty, *Lodge*, 391–401, and on the 1920 campaign, see Wesley M. Bagby, *The Road to Normalcy: The Presidential Campaign and Election of 1920* (Baltimore: Johns Hopkins University Press, 1962).

29. Josephus Daniels diary, October 6, 1919, *Wilson Papers* 63: 555; Grayson memorandum, October 6, 1919, ibid., 496. On the background of this cabinet meeting, which included discussions with Tumulty and Grayson, see Lansing desk diary, October 3, 1919, ibid., 547, and Lansing memorandum, February 23, 1920, ibid. 64: 455–56. Tumulty recalled those earlier discussions as a heated exchange between Lansing, who wanted to remove Wilson, and himself, who loyally defended his chief. See Tumulty, *Woodrow Wilson as I Know Him* (Garden City, N.Y.: Doubleday, Page & Co., 1921), 443–44. There is strong reason to doubt Tumulty's version, although Lansing was not on good terms with Wilson.

30. *New York Times*, December 6, 1919. For eyewitness accounts of the meeting, see E. Wilson notes, [December 5, 1919], *Wilson Papers* 64: 133–35, and Grayson memorandum, December 5, 1919, ibid., 135–39. Unfortunately, these accounts do not support Mrs. Wilson's later version in which Fall allegedly said, "Well, Mr. President, we have all been praying for you," and Wilson supposedly shot back, "Which way, Senator?" E. Wilson, *My Memoir*, 299. On this point see editors' observation, *Wilson Papers* 64: 135 n. 2.

31. A few handicapped persons have achieved some political prominence since Roosevelt. Charles Potter, who lost both legs in World War II and walked on artificial legs with the aid of canes, served a term in the Senate from Michigan in the 1950s. Daniel Inouye, who lost an arm in World War II, has served in

Congress from Hawaii since its statehood, first as a representative and since 1963 as a senator. John Swainson, who used braces and canes because of polio, served a term as governor of Michigan in the 1960s. Another "polio," John Collins, served as mayor of Boston. Max Cleland, who lost both legs and an arm in Vietnam and uses a wheelchair, headed the Veterans Administration in the 1970s and currently serves as secretary of state of Georgia. Two senators, Robert Dole of Kansas, whose right hand was crippled as a result of wounds in World War II, and Robert Kerrey of Nebraska, who lost a leg in Vietnam, have recently sought their parties' presidential nominations. None of these men evidently made any effort to conceal his handicap, and Collins used crutches as a campaign symbol. Neither of the presidential nominees in 1992 had an immediately noticeable handicap.

32. Baker diary, January 23, 1920, *Wilson Papers* 64: 321.

The Expanding White House:

Creating the East
and West Wings

Robert H. Ferrell

In libraries across the country, with their processions of steel stacks, stand the rows of books about the White House. Yet those rows do not tell us much. With all due respect to the mansion's great rooms, most books fail to make the point that throughout the nineteenth century the business of the executive branch of the government of the United States was conducted on the second floor, often in shabby circumstances unforgettable to anyone entering the house. Nor do they say much about how, in 1902, all this changed with the construction of a so-called temporary office building to the west of the mansion, and of how this building underwent an enlargement in 1909, a disastrous fire in 1929, and another enlargement in 1934. White House histories do not mention the construction of the East Wing during World War II, nor the fact that after the war the offices spilled over into the old State, War, and Navy Building, renamed the Executive Office Building.[1]

The books — a plague on most of them — do not relate that from the beginning the presidency has been more than a single elected personage housed in a mansion. It has been a group of individuals, in recent years a vast, uncounted group, working away in the wings, or under the huge mansard roof and behind the pilaster.

I

The few serious books about life and government in the White House inform us that the business of the executive branch dominated the mansion even in the nineteenth century, before the wings were built. Government was simpler then, the country much smaller in size and population, reaching to California only in 1848, to a population of 100 million in the Wilson presidency just before our entry into World War I. Small government was the rule. Still, even in those antediluvian years, the executive branch operated out of the White House with a presence that no president or his family could forget.

Photographs are the best way to sense how the mansion looked when the executive offices were in the building, not in the wings or across the street. They show that after the Civil War, the executive offices on the east side of the second floor were nothing short of a mess. "Conversion" was the word to describe them: everything was converted. Bedchambers and dressing rooms had been converted, and the signs of conversion were the fireplaces, the long windows, the ornamental wood. Then there was the lighting — gaslights were converted in 1891 to receptacles for the new Edison filaments. Years later, when Charles F. McKim redid the mansion, he found burned-out places where the bare wires had blackened the wood. What McKim, with his reverence for the distant past, identified as relics of the fire of 1814 was the more prosaic work of the lighting system. The appearance of the lights was bad enough. It perfectly matched the bedrooms, where wires ran in a maze and bulbs loomed out of glasses for the gaslights. No wonder President McKinley, working evenings in his study, preferred to work by gaslight rather than try the electric lights.

Nearly everything in the offices was makeshift. Telephones came in during the Hayes administration — a simple time when, in the evenings, the president answered the phone himself. The big speakers with their anchored receivers stood on office desks, cords rising to the heavens, straight up to where someone affixed them to Hoban's plaster before taking them across the ceilings. Against walls stood flat tables stacked with gilded "in" boxes and papers and glassed-in cases for ledgers and more papers. The floors were covered with old-fashioned Brussels carpeting, wall to wall, with throw rugs over worn areas.

In the photographs are no spittoons or ashtrays, which is unbelievable. Someone must have gathered them up and put them out of sight. A perpetual smell of tobacco, chewed and smoked, must have filled the working rooms clustered at one end of the floor that contained, at its other end, the rooms of the president and his family.

The operation of the offices has been recorded. President McKinley, almost never without a cigar, worked away wearily signing army and navy commissions. "Let's get busy," he would say to his correspondence clerk, Ira R. T. Smith, a young man who had come to Washington from East Liverpool, Ohio, at the recommendation of his uncle, a wealthy pottery manufacturer. Smith left the White House in the time of President Truman and spent his last days in Santa Barbara, California, but never forgot the McKinley era. The president would start in on the commissions, humming a Methodist tune that gave him the courage to face the task. Smith would hand him a commission from the pile, the president would sign it, and Smith would put it on a table to dry. Each commission was made of sheepskin and was impossible to blot, so he would spread them out over all the desks in the presidential office, and thereafter on the floor. "Something ought to be done about this," McKinley would complain. "Somebody else ought to be able to sign these."[2]

When McKinley worked in his office near the oval room upstairs, with the cabinet room nearby, half a dozen secretaries, known then as clerks, grouped themselves in the offices, supervised by a single presidential secretary. McKinley's was John Addison Porter, pince-nezed, portly, self-important, and choleric; he was followed by George B. Cortelyou, less impressive but more efficient. Both men were trying, self-consciously, to follow the path of Cleveland's first secretary, Daniel S. Lamont, who had become secretary of war. Cortelyou stayed into the Theodore Roosevelt years, but the importance of presidential secretaries diminished with the removal of their office to the West Wing in 1902. Few people know that Cortelyou's successor, really an office manager, was William Loeb of the *Manchester Union Leader*. Charles D. Norton, appointed by President Taft in 1910, was informally called assistant to the president, which more accurately describes his job. Wilson revived the practice of having the secretary as an important figure with Joseph

The clutter of newly added telephone wires and electrical cords in a late nineteenth-century White House office appears vividly in this photograph by Frances Benjamin Johnston. Courtesy of the Library of Congress.

P. Tumulty. Harding did the same with George Christian, and then secretaries again diminished in dignity, turning formally into assistants.

During McKinley's first year, the upstairs executive offices functioned fairly well despite the chaotic atmosphere. The Spanish-American War demonstrated that these rooms were too small, cramped, and inefficient for the work of the presidency. Pressure for change came first from overcrowding, then from the ambitions of Colonel Theodore Bingham, the new keeper of the presidential building and grounds, and then from President Theodore Roosevelt's six children, who, despite the workers on the second floor, sought to take over that part of their parents' house.

The Spanish-American War brought the first pressure for change. The telegraph key chattered day and night, and maps of Cuba and the Philippines cluttered the walls. Uniformed officers strode in and out of the offices. It was all reminiscent of the Civil War, which must have pleased old Colonel William H. Crook, who handled White House and executive accounts. Crook had never gotten over the fact that for a few brief months he had been one of Lincoln's bodyguards. By this time the colonel, who perhaps was a breveted lieutenant (no former military man present in the White House at this time, save for Major McKinley, seems to have borne a rank lower than colonel), was a wizened little man with a half-beard who spent time taking visitors through the rooms below and reminisced about the evening when President Lincoln, en route to Ford's Theater, failed to wish him the usual good night.[3]

The entrance to the executive offices during these years was by a crooked staircase that looked like the stairs of a second-class hotel — straight banisters, stairs carpeted, people constantly moving up and down. At the top, in the corridor, the reporters loitered, the hum of their voices audible in the president's office nearby. McKinley's White House offered reporters none of the facilities they enjoy there today, not even telephones. When news of the sinking of the *Maine*, of the battles of Manila Bay and Santiago Bay, of Shafter's taking the surrender of the Spanish forces came over the wire, journalists tumbled down the stairs to give their dispatches to bicycle messengers who pedaled off as fast as they could to their newspapers.[4]

The Spanish-American War was the first force that moved the executive offices out of the second floor into their own building. The second was Colonel Bingham, who in 1897 took charge of the Office of Public Buildings and Grounds. Bingham's organizational skills eventually eliminated the need for the role he enjoyed, but for several years he was a presence to be reckoned with. Colonel Bingham wanted to get the executive offices out of the White House and arranged a scheme for doing so. President Harrison's wife had envisioned buildings on each side of the White House that would have created a miniature Versailles. It may have been the increasing number of mansions in Washington that persuaded her to enlarge the White House. The changing architectural ideas of the time, in particular the move from gothic to classical themes, may have played a part. But the major reason was the need for more space for their extended family. Nothing came of her venture. In 1893, Colonel John M. Wilson, then the custodian of the White House and its grounds, suggested an office wing on the west terrace facing the State, War, and Navy Building. This simple solution did not inspire Bingham, who chose, instead, a design more restrained than Mrs. Harrison's and much more unrestrained than Wilson's. On both sides of the mansion he envisioned circular, colonnaded, domed buildings that would have dwarfed the main structure, each having a grand entrance with many steps. He unveiled this proposal in December 1900 before President McKinley and a large group of celebrants of the White House centennial.

Bingham's plan lost out for several reasons. For one, he held professional architects in contempt and did not keep his thoughts to himself. He celebrated their architectural failures. "I can tell you of a number of cases," he wrote. "The average Congressman says, 'to hell with art.' . . . If the White House is to be extended in the immediate future, I venture to say that the only way will be to take my plan, appropriate money to carry it out, directing and authorizing me to have it criticized by architects 'of conspicuous ability,' leaving the final decisions in the hands of the Chief of Engineers, U.S. Army."[5] In a few words, Bingham insulted every architect in the United States. He also insulted the landscape architects when he asked the illustrious building architect David H. Burnham to come from Chicago to Washington to confer with him, but then changed his mind with a telegram, sent to Burnham on the east-bound train, telling him to return home. If this were not enough, he got together with some friends from the Corps of Engineers and proposed a road right down the middle of the Mall. The architects and landscape planners conspired to undermine Bingham's project. Senator James McMillan of Michigan, chairman of the White House Centennial Committee, joined them.

If there was another reason for the failure, it was McKinley's wife, Ida. A beautiful young woman when she married her handsome major, she had succumbed to a malady that was never defined. Nervous, semi-invalid, Mrs. McKinley spent almost all her time in her room. She insisted that there would be "no hammering" while she was in the White House.[6]

Although Bingham's plan failed, the impossibility of keeping the executive offices upstairs at the White House became thoroughly obvious shortly after McKinley's assassination. Previous arrangements had been possible in part because of the small size of presidential families. Cleveland married Frances Folsom, and baby Ruth was born, followed by other children, but this was in his second term. The Harrisons had also been crowded in the White House with both a son and daughter and both their young families — including a grandson of the president, known as Baby McKee, who tiresomely crawled across the pages of the country's newspapers. The childless McKinleys did not require much space. But for the Roosevelts, the offices were impossible — the family of six children needed the entire second floor. There was a single guest bedroom. The residential part of the floor contained two bathrooms, one for the presidential bedroom, the other for all the others.

Young Ethel Roosevelt dramatized the need for expansion. One Sunday, Ethel came into the executive offices swinging a stick cut off a tree, walked up to the chief telegrapher and telephone operator, James Smithers, who was reading a newspaper and had his feet on the desk, and demanded, "Smithers, put up the tennis net for me." Smithers paid no attention. "Did you hear me?" she demanded. When Smithers said he could not leave his post, young Ethel raised her stick and struck Smithers on the shins, cutting his leg. Smithers seized Ethel, turned her across his lap, and spanked her. She protested, and just then Smithers looked up and saw the president standing in the doorway watching. Roosevelt

Colonel Theodore Bingham's monumental scheme for an expanded White House was never implemented. Subsequent additions have kept the original structure as the center of focus. Courtesy of the National Park Service.

walked over, seized Ethel by the shoulder, put her out the door, and said to her, "Didn't I tell you never to come in these offices?"[7]

The mansion itself provided the other reasons to move: it needed refurbishing because of impossible electrical apparatus, insufficient plumbing, sagging floors, and five layers of wallpaper. When President Arthur auctioned some of the house's contents, someone bought the rat trap that caught the rat that ate President Lincoln's suit, but the rat's relatives remained in residence. Then there was Arthur's Tiffany colored-glass screen in the front entrance. When Roosevelt asked what was to become of it, architect McKim suggested dynamite.[8] For all these reasons, it was decided during the restoration to move the offices to a newly built "temporary" West Wing, retaining in the mansion only the president's public office, which Roosevelt used chiefly for special occasions.

II

June 20, 1902, was a historic day for the White House. Congress appropriated $540,641 for remodeling the mansion, including $65,196 for a separate office building. This structure, admittedly temporary, became the first of several buildings known as the West Wing. It was to be constructed "with sufficient foundation, and walls suitable for a durable permanent building, and of sufficient strength for an additional story when needed."

But to get the offices out of the White House into the new building, it was necessary to get something else out of the way first: the series of greenhouses, erected between 1857 and 1885, which separated the mansion from the State, War, and Navy Building. It was necessary, as Roosevelt said, to "smash the glass houses!"

The Republican Roosevelt might have seemed the man for the task. Still, removing the greenhouses required more diplomacy than the president imagined. It was one thing to give a contract to McKim, Mead, and White to redo the White House and build an office structure. It was something else to get the space to do it. The canny Colonel Bingham saw an opening and moved directly to take on his enemies, the architects and planners, headed by the New Yorker, McKim. He pointed out to Mrs. Roosevelt that if there were no greenhouses, there would be no

A view of the White House from the west with the greenhouses, removed in 1902, in the foreground. Courtesy of the Historical Society of Washington, D.C.

flowers to decorate the White House and send to friends and callers, which had been the custom for years. The White House without flowers! That would be bad enough. To fill in the flower gap, the Roosevelts (who, despite their opulent tastes and acquaintance with high living, were not really rich) might have to pay for the flowers themselves.

Ike Hoover, the erstwhile electrician and White House chief usher, remembered the greenhouses with considerable affection, and so described them in his book, one of the few volumes of White House reminiscences that says anything valuable.[9] Next to the mansion stood a tall glass house known as the conservatory, directly over the west terrace that President Jefferson had constructed, along with an east terrace, to set off the mansion from the grounds sloping down toward what later became the Ellipse. Next to the conservatory stood a big greenhouse, and beyond it a two-row house and a rounded-end house, like a U. To the south of the big greenhouse lay a house in the form of a shed, sloped down to the south. From it protruded a handsome entrance, perhaps for the greenhouse keeper. Hoover was a young man when he came to the mansion and easily remembered the "dear old conservatory" because couples roamed there during parties and lost themselves among the palms and ferns. Apart from this use, it was a place to put the United States Marine Band, then under the baton of John Philip Sousa. From the conservatory, "Sousie" and his men, scarlet coats standing out against the greenery, sent his famous marches soaring through the house. Hoover also remembered the "funny kinds of plants": dwarf tropical fruit trees bearing bananas, oranges, lemons, figs, and nuts; artillery plants with blossoms that burst and sent out vaporous clouds like cannons; fly-catching plants with leaves that curled up when tickled in the middle. The other greenhouses contained roses, carnations, orchids, camellias, and — during the Cleveland presidency — a pansy house for the president's winsome young wife, who adored pansies.

Given all these attractions, including the rubber plants that tobacco chewers admired (Captain John J. Pershing could kill a good rubber plant in three weeks), Bingham saw his chance. He got Mrs. Roosevelt's ear, who got the president's ear, who wrote back to Bingham: "Please tell Mr. McKim that this is absolutely essential. The green house *must* be provided for."[10]

McKim was up to the challenge. He detested greenhouses as relics of everything he hated in architecture, including the ability to ruin a house's prospect.[11] He traveled to Oyster Bay, where he received the president's approval not to smash the glass houses, but only to move them. The iron, hence movable, greenhouses would still protect the plants, but somewhere else.[12]

McKim then got down to business. More than three hundred workmen turned the White House upside down. Meanwhile, McKim arranged a new place of business for the executive offices, as well as reconstructing the east terrace, which contained coatrooms, umbrella stands, and other new conveniences (toilets), all fronted by a porte cochere. After the 1902 reconstruction, the north entrance of the mansion became the private entrance. The south entrance was for occupants and guests. The east entrance, where people entered the house through the basement, climbing stairs to the entertainment rooms, was for social occasions. The west entrance was for the offices, restricted to the business that had plagued inhabitants of the mansion.

McKim's temporary office building was made of brick and painted white. Although a simple box in outline, it was carefully put together, with a series of long windows and short ones above, much like the federal-style houses of a half-century earlier. According to a statement to Congress when the appropriation came before the Senate, "The temporary building would include: a Cabinet room, President's office and retiring room, offices for two secretaries, a telegraph and telephone room, a large room for the stenographers, a room for the press, a main hall to be fitted as a reception room, file rooms and closets in the basement."[13] Secretary Cortelyou reported, with understatement, that with the exception of the historic cabinet table and two or three chairs, none of the furniture in the executive offices was suitable for removal, and, in the appropriation, $10,000 was reserved for furniture. The executive offices were finished September 30 and occupied, after allowing for the wood to dry, in mid-October. As McKim's architect friend Charles Moore described the new situation, the president ceased to "live over the shop."[14] If he did not gain privacy, he gained opportunity for privacy — the choice was his.

For students of the presidency, it is important to remark that the enlarged White House, as historian William Seale has put it, enabled Roosevelt "to make the White House his stage. On it he would make his life a performance dramatizing himself and his ideas."[15]

The president's suite in the new building looked, Seale writes, like the double parlor in a large private house. The north room, the larger of the two, was for cabinet meetings. Directly behind, to the south, lay the president's room. Sliding doors divided the two and usually stood open. Two large fireplaces lent intimacy to the suite. The president often held small weekly receptions here instead of in the East Room.

The Theodore Roosevelt years, so wondrously emblazoned on the history of the country, as he hoped they would be, were often lived out in the Executive Mansion. It was there that he chose to conduct his more important conferences, lending the dignity of the McKim restoration to whatever he had in mind. Still, when one looks at the wonderfully clear photograph of Roosevelt standing in Prince Albert attire beside a huge globe, creases on his pant legs bespeaking excellent work by the White House valets, it is impossible to forget what he must have looked like as he strode between the two fireplaces in the double-parlor–like office. There hardly was need for him to take important visitors to the White House.

One function that Roosevelt may have had in mind for the executive offices, which he used to the utmost as soon as he moved in, was to court the newspaper press. Roosevelt played with the humors of the reporters, walking out among them on the slightest impulse and conversing. This he could do in the small, newly established press room to the right of the front entrance of the West Wing. Whatever was on his mind, he was good copy, with his exaggerated words and, one can even imagine, a bit of his oratorical gesture of pounding his right hand, fingers together in a fist, into his cupped left hand.[16]

When the offices moved into the West Wing, there was a second, unexpected change in dealing with the press. The front entrance of the remodeled White House, which closed off, save for special occasions, use of the old staircase (indeed, McKim replaced the latter with a great state staircase), made it possible for reporters to play a game that continues to the present day. When all the offices were in the mansion, all visitors to the president were easy to see, coming and going, for they

The last remnant of the greenhouses juts out between the White House and the Executive Office Building (now referred to as the West Wing), shown under construction in this 1902 photograph. Courtesy of the Library of Congress.

entered on the north and climbed the stairs. Beginning in 1902, they could slip in through the social entrance on the south and continue through the ground floor corridor, unnoticed by the press, and along the colonnade of the West Wing into the president's office. This became the famous rear entrance about which so many people spoke. The press corps was now required to keep a vigil in the press room and lobby, noting with care any visitors of importance and watching for clues to visitors who came in the private way.

In one respect, Roosevelt may have erred in how he dealt with the press from his new West Wing. For some of his successors, it became an egregious error. In the past it had been customary for cabinet members to stop on the north portico or driveway after meetings to talk over with the press what they had said upstairs to the president. Roosevelt detested these breaches of confidentiality and addressed the cabinet about them three times. Decades later President Truman deeply resented it when cabinet members or other officials, after visiting him in the Oval Office, went outside and virtually held press conferences in which they told everything that went on. Lecturing his cabinet against the practice — which became much easier when reporters could sally from the press room at the entrance to the executive offices or pursue officials up or down West Executive Avenue — Theodore Roosevelt was really putting himself at the front of national news. For other, less adroit chief executives, this could mean the possibility of blame, rather than praise, when things went wrong. In some measure, lower officials are the president's lightning rods for errors — as Franklin Roosevelt once told his postmaster general, Frank C. Walker.[17]

III

Much has happened to the executive offices since Theodore Roosevelt departed. Major physical changes occurred under Presidents William H. Taft, Herbert Hoover, and Franklin Roosevelt, and it is fairly easy to describe them. In terms of work, nothing less than the history of the executive branch of the government of the United States since the year 1909 would be required to describe what has happened there.

Taft created an oval office — not today's room but a similar office in a different part of the West Wing. Taft placed this in the center of the south wall of the building after he enlarged McKim's temporary building. In a second enlargement, Franklin Roosevelt moved the Oval Office to the southeast corner of the West Wing, where it remains. Taft remodeled the building and occupied his new office in October 1909. He changed the building from a staff office into an office for the president. The cabinet room also lay in the new addition, to the east, with the secretary's rooms to the west. In some ways Taft's dealings with his staff helped restore the camaraderie that existed when everyone was in the White House up on the second floor. Taft was in the office every day and dealt closely with his office workers. But in another way, he ended the familial nature of the offices. In private, Taft was hardly the jovial, warm individual he appeared to be in public; his feet hurt, he ate too much, and he often fell asleep and snored at his desk. Moreover, he subjected the staff to his assistant, Charles Norton, whom Ira Smith found nearly intolerable. When the overly efficient, officious Norton left to become vice president of a New York bank, the office staff gathered at the door, and as he went out, the group hummed the Doxology.[18]

President Woodrow Wilson was a different personality, by no means so often at his desk. He worked three or four hours a day, and frequently preferred his upstairs office, which meant that his Hammond typewriter had to be transported back and forth. At the outset the president did not quite know what to make of his sizable staff, thirty-five to forty people. Upon coming into the Oval Office he was apt to pick up unanswered letters from desks, taking them into the office and typing replies himself. An expert stenographer, he sometimes took his own notes rather than using secretaries ready and willing to help.

Ira Smith recalled that when Warren G. Harding was president, a letter came from New York, written in a feminine hand, followed by another. He took them to the president's secretary, George Christian, who opened them to find pleas for money accompanied by the lady's assertions that her child had been sired by the president himself. Smith's job was to handle mail, and Harding already had upbraided him for opening what the president said was personal correspondence. Christian took the letters from New York, tore them into long strips, tore them again, and placed them in a wastebasket. Years later Smith encountered Christian at a White House gathering. Harding's secretary had gone blind, but he recognized the sound of Smith's voice. He told Smith it was fortunate he had disposed of those letters.[19]

Calvin Coolidge, a fine administrator, was accustomed to sitting in the Oval Office and annotating mail with commentaries that his secretary and clerks filled out into full-fledged, nice-sounding letters. The president from New England, laconic to a fault, would sit at his desk, feet on top, smoking a Havana cigar (he gave White Owls to callers), writing "Yes" or "No" in a bold black hand. Of a delegation of female peace workers who Secretary of State Charles Evans Hughes suggested with mock formality should be received in the Oval Office, he wrote "Let 'em call."[20]

Under Hoover came a revolution in efficiency as thorough as Norton's during the Taft era. The president began to employ three secretaries instead of one. Each required a presentable office with a smaller room for a stenographer. The staff also grew, which put pressure on available space. Forty people had been working in five rooms, with the second floor of the West Wing only an attic and the basement usable for naught save storage. After Hoover's changes, the staff numbered well over one hundred.

Then occurred the disastrous fire of Christmas Eve, 1929, which burned almost everything in the West Wing or ruined it with water from the fire hoses. Firemen had their machinery on West Executive Avenue, and, unfortunately, the worst of the flames were in the building's north part. The president's dinner companions joined the work of taking files out onto the snow-covered grounds. Pictures were removed from walls, books from shelves. The president's younger son, Allan, home from college, went into the Oval Office and helped remove drawers from his father's desk. Ike Hoover covered the cabinet table with a wet tarpaulin.

After the fire the offices were rebuilt without large changes. The Great Depression had begun, a bad time for such projects, in Hoover's view. Back in his office, Hoover worked as hard as he could, humorless to the end, largely unable to deflect the economic disaster. One moment of mirth during that time occurred when the president's cabinet, assembled in their room that looked southward onto a flat area used by White House servants as a drying place for laundry, saw presidential linen that included the First Lady's panties. There was a snicker around the table, silence on the part of the president. Thereafter presidential laundry was sent out elsewhere.[21]

During Franklin Roosevelt's administration, the West Wing received its third reconstruction, following upon those of 1909 (the Oval Office) and 1930 (after the fire). During World War II, Roosevelt arranged for the construction of the East Wing, replacing McKim's cloak room (informally dubbed the "Hat Box") and porte cochere.

In the beginning it was uncertain how the old-timer Charles Moore, McKim's friend, who was by then the seventy-eight-year-old chairman of the United States Fine Arts Commission, would take the idea of reconstruction. Moore had written a biography of McKim, whom he revered. Roosevelt sent an emissary, his uncle Frederick Delano, to lay the plans before Moore. Moore wanted instead to tear down the West Wing and place the executive offices in the State, War, and Navy Building, turning that hulking relic into a Greek temple like the Treasury Building on the other side. He would connect the new offices to the White House with a tunnel. Delano got nowhere and told his nephew so.

Moore was partially accommodated. Construction began on the building in March 1934 and was completed by November. The result was a vastly enlarged building that adhered closely to McKim's original design by raising the roof to provide a workable second floor and by constructing a basement warren of offices that extended almost magically under the grass to the south and received light from a well in the center of the underground area. Most of the changes were thus invisible. West Executive Avenue also was lowered to bring in light.

The most important change was a shifting of the Oval Office from the center of the former West Wing to the southeast corner of the new one, where it has remained until the present day. Hence all Oval Office photographs before August 1934 are not of the nerve center of government that we now know so well. One might contend that the new Oval Office lacks the functional prominence of the old, that it really belongs in the center, not off to one side. The advantage of the present location is its very remoteness, for this gives the president a privacy that no central office could offer. The entire building, despite enlargement, is no gigantic place; it is still small, as corporate executive offices go. Like the remote Oval Office, it too gives the president the opportunity to work undisturbed by the increasing reportage of modern journalism. From waiting rooms a visitor approaches the president's office through a series of halls, ending in a small antechamber. Inside, the office is quiet and removed, connecting only with the cabinet room and the office of the president's secretary. French doors open onto a porch and an extension south of the colonnade. In summer the greenery and blooms of the Rose Garden provide the chief executive with a peaceful haven in which to work and think.

The architect of the Rooseveltian rearrangement, Eric Gugler of New York, received much praise for his work, including a letter from Moore:

> It was a great satisfaction to go over the new White House Office Building. The fundamentals have been taken care of in most satisfactory manner. You have gained the additional space needed at the least possible expense of the none too abundant areas of the grounds. Moreover, you have kept the spirit of the White House throughout. . . . And you have preserved the charm that Hoban and Latrobe imparted to the original house and that McKim added to when he made it into a residence for the First Gentlemen of the Nation.[22]

World War II saw almost no changes in the West Wing other than the presence of military guards in the halls and the installation of bulletproof glass in the lower part of the Oval Office windows. But it did see the hurried construction of the first East Wing, asked for by the president on the day after Pearl Harbor. It was finished in May 1942, in a rough way, with interiors completed only on the second floor. First-floor walls had no plastering, only tan cloth covers. Final interior finishing came after the war, with the rooms done in wood.

Two other wartime innovations involving the executive offices were the secret bomb shelter and the Map Room. The former was a remarkable place, with seven-foot-thick walls and a nine-foot-thick ceiling of concrete reinforced by steel. A large room, forty feet square, it contained an island-like presidential bedroom and bath, with walls three feet thick. Anything coming through the ceiling would have to penetrate nine feet, and from the sides, ten. Side rooms contained toilets, storage areas for food and water, and machinery for ventilation. In the common room would be the principal presidential assistants, provided with telephones and telegraphic and radio equipment.

The Map Room was something else. In terms of White House organization it marked a throwback to the pre-1902 era, for it was in the basement of the mansion, next to the White House doctor's office, convenient to the president's route from the oval room to the Oval Office; to get there he only had to be wheeled from the elevator across the hall. The Map Room held all the paraphernalia of military command. Here officers, including the youthful George Elsey, took round-the-clock shifts. Here Elsey arranged an ingenious personal memento by having Roosevelt and British Prime Minister Winston Churchill sign a Bruce Rogers poster containing the text of the Atlantic Charter. This is the only signed text of that well-known document.

In 1945 the Roosevelt era came to a sudden end, when the president suffered a fatal stroke on April 12. With Harry S Truman in the Oval Office, the presidency moved away from the grand seigneur tradition of the Roosevelts. (Theodore Roosevelt had objected to walking past the servants' quarters on his way to the executive offices.)[23] Truman, like Coolidge, separated himself from the great office he held and made fun of "Potomac fever," an ailment that afflicted people in Washington, especially assistants in the executive offices, who felt the aura of McKim's First Gentlemen restoration. The thirty-third president of the United States sometimes recorded the symptoms in random diary jottings. "Some of my boys who came in with me," he wrote on June 1, 1945, "are having trouble with their dignity and prerogatives. It's hell when a man gets in close association with the President. Something happens to him. . . . That publicity complex is hell and few can escape it here. When a good man comes along who hasn't the bug I try to grab him."[24]

Truman inaugurated what one might describe as the modern presidency, in that big government became the norm in Washington. The war centralized many things, but postwar problems with Russia made foreign policy a chief focus of the nation, even in peacetime. The nation and the world wanted political leadership. The rapidly increasing size of the staff of the executive offices reflected this. Truman knew that even with the completed East Wing he could not possibly run the executive branch with the office space available. In his forthright manner, he directed White House architect Lorenzo S. Winslow to make sketches for an addition to the West Wing, 15,000 square feet to the south, including an auditorium, press space, more offices, and a staff cafeteria. Mainly, he had to get the reporters, often two hundred of them, out of the Oval Office, where they pushed the fragile furniture around, spattered the fine carpet with ink from fountain pens, dropped and stomped on cigarettes, and created a mess at every press conference. The doors were so small that the self-appointed dean of the press corps, Merriman Smith, who in some part deserved what happened to him, broke his leg trying to get out of the place.

The modern American presidency did not attract an iota of sympathy from Congress. The Republican majority refused the president's proposed expansion, and Truman's only recourse was to send staff members across the street to the State, War, and Navy Building when the State Department moved out in 1947. For a while the place became a rabbit warren, but finally it was cleaned up, and its architecture was appreciated. In all its mansard splendor, it became, like the wings, an essential part of the executive branch.

Being separated from the West Wing, where the president has his office, the staff members in the East Wing have been inordinately independent ever since their building rose out of the debris of the old McKim social entrance. In Franklin Roosevelt's presidency, powerful people, such as James F. Byrnes, the president's principal assistant, and Samuel I. Rosenman, the president's speech writer, known grandiloquently as his special counsel, had offices there. Rivalry soon developed about who would work on the second floor and who on the first. When one of Roosevelt's secretaries, Marvin McIntyre, died, Sam Rosenman pounced on his first-floor office. Within one day he had it fumigated and moved in. This earned him the enmity of the president's correspondence secretary, William D. Hassett, who felt himself entitled to a first-floor office. A hard worker, Hassett was the composer of countless "valentines" to retiring officials and individuals who wished to celebrate Love Your Dog Week. He disgustedly described Rosenman as a "squatter." Both men became carryovers into the Truman administration. In mid-June of 1945, a choice first-floor corner office became available. It was vacated by one of Truman's World War I friends, Edward D. McKim (no relation to the architect), who came with the new president and stayed only a few weeks until an attack of Potomac fever nearly killed him, and there was nothing for Truman to do but send him on a special mission to Pope Pius XII. When the president gave Hassett the office, it contained Mc-Kim's deluxe desk. As soon as the morning staff meeting of June 16 was over and Hassett and Rosenman had repaired to the East Wing, Rosenman called Hassett up and asked for the desk. Hassett grumpily said no. To a friend in the West Wing he expressed his astonishment at the chutzpah of the East Wing. Everyone in the East Wing had wanted to change to the West Wing. Byrnes, Rosenman, and Hassett all would have fumigated themselves out of their offices in an instant if they could have worked in closer proximity to the president.

The White House offices have not changed much since the days of Harry Truman. Only once did a serious problem arise in their operation; this involved a confusion about federal jurisdiction in 1977. The trouble arose when some White House mice, after asserting their personalities elsewhere, sought to take over the Oval Office. President Carter engaged the resources of the General Services Administration, which diminished the population, but a mouse, perhaps more than one, had the bad taste to expire in the wall of the president's office. The president requested immediate action, but the G.S.A. declared its responsibility ended at the inside wall. The National Park Service then received an appeal but declared its responsibility ended on the outside wall. The president rose up in wrath, after which someone solved the problem.

In recent years the Carter mouse problem was the most untoward office management crisis to occur in the West Wing. If there were others, they all must have been connected with Ira Smith's activities as opener of presidential mail. Part of Smith's trouble was the sheer increase in the volume of mail. He had begun in McKinley's time with a hundred letters a day, which seemed a torrent. By the time of the Truman administration, he was getting 150,000 letters, cards, and packages a day. The increase started with the picture-postcard craze shortly after the turn of the century ("Wish you were here," wrote the card people). It worsened markedly in 1934 with the March of Dimes, hundreds of thousands of which marched into the executive offices one or more at a time, including the dime that had a hole in the middle and a string and label attached directing it to the White House. Smith especially loathed dimes stuck with Scotch tape, for the Treasury would not accept taped dimes; it took fire-extinguisher fluid to get the tape off. Then there were the chickens during the Truman administration. When the president asked all Americans to have chickenless Thursdays, his request inspired farmers to send him crates of live chickens. Perhaps the most amusing of Smith's stories concerned the letter from a war widow seeking a pension and enclosing a sample of her husband's ashes to prove it. A clerk, Smith wrote, inadvertently opened the letter in front of an electric fan, and the evidence vanished.

And so, in the White House wings and across the street in the renamed Executive Office Building work the president's approximately fifteen hundred assistants — no one knows the exact number — deputized by cabinet departments and other offices. Clearly, they are not just another bureaucracy. They use the magical stationery, and, when they make their telephone calls, they remind common citizens of the power that is far away, yet near: "The White House is calling." Mostly for their work, sometimes, one suspects, to impress the people they call, they adopt the aura of the building. But this is entirely fitting and proper, for by retaining the executive offices, the White House has become a symbol, a visible sign, a wondrously chaste vision, of the authority that surrounds the executive branch of the great government of the United States.

NOTES

1. All students of the White House are indebted to the historian William Seale and to his definitive work, *The President's House: A History*, 2 vols. (Washington: White House Historical Association, 1986). As he so correctly relates of the mansion and its inhabitants, "Through the White House past, those who have known the most usually wrote the least." Seale, *President's House*, 2:721.

2. Ira R. T. Smith, *"Dear Mr. President . . .": The Story of Fifty Years in the White House Mail Room* (New York: Julian Messner, 1949), 35–36.

3. "'Mr. Crook,' he said, kindly but firmly, 'you have had a long, hard day's work already, and must go home to sleep and rest. I cannot afford to have you get all tired out and exhausted.' It was then that he neglected, for the first and only time, to say good-night to me. Instead, he turned, with his kind, grave face, and said: 'Good-bye, Crook,' and went into his room. I thought of it at the moment; and a few hours later, when the awful news flashed over Washington."

Memories of the White House: The Home Life of Our Presidents from Lincoln to Roosevelt (Boston: Little, Brown & Co., 1911), 40.

4. The night before Cleveland underwent a secret operation for cancer of the mouth, aboard the yacht *Oneida,* he complained bitterly to the assembled physicians that the ever-present office seekers appeared to him in his dreams. They all used the stairs to the second floor. As Esther Singleton, an early chronicler of the White House, wrote, quoting Colonel John M. Wilson, in charge of the mansion and grounds, "The public stairway at the east side of the mansion never looked shabbier than it has lately. The army that passed over it since March left indelible marks. The staircase has been painted and varnished, and begins to make a much better appearance." Esther Singleton, *The Story of the White House,* 2 vols. (New York: McClure, 1907), 2:238. But even during Republican administrations the same problem was present. Singleton, quoting E. V. Smalley, offered a description of the short-lived Garfield administration: "The atmosphere is close and heavy on this stairway and affects one singularly. Perhaps the sighs of the disappointed office-seekers who for more than half a century have descended the steps, have permeated the walls and give to the air a quality that defies ventilation. There are crowds in the ante-room and crowds in the upper hall. All these people are eager-eyed, restless and nervous. They want something which the great man in that well-guarded room across the hall can give if he chooses, but which they fear they will not get." Ibid. 2:168–69.

5. Seale, *President's House,* 2:654.

6. Charles Moore, *The Life and Times of Charles Follen McKim* (Boston: Houghton Mifflin Co., 1929), 204.

7. Smith, *"Dear Mr. President,"* 57–58.

8. "It is said," wrote the witty Moore, "that the screen followed the White House sideboard to a saloon — a remarkable coincidence in the operation of the law of gravitation." Moore, *McKim,* 221.

9. Irwin Hood Hoover, *Forty-two Years in the White House* (Boston: Houghton Mifflin Co., 1934), 5.

10. Letter of June 28, 1902, quoted in William Ryan and Desmond Guinness, *The White House: An Architectural History* (New York: McGraw-Hill, 1980), 154.

11. Ryan and Guinness amusingly describe the greenhouses as "a giant fungus." They relate that the conservatory was decorated with twelve stained-glass picture windows made by P. Klaus of Baltimore — a sight that must have brought Charles McKim to the verge of apoplexy. Ibid., 137.

12. "It is understood that the iron or steel portion of the greenhouses now occupying space on the west terrace shall be removed and set up in the White House grounds on the location which shall least interfere with the view from the house. Whatever additional space may be deemed necessary by the President shall be provided in greenhouses to be constructed in connection with the Prop-

agating Gardens but to be known as the White House Conservatories." Moore, *McKim*, opposite p. 216.

13. Singleton, *Story of the White House*, 2:292.

14. Moore, *McKim*, 220.

15. Seale, *President's House*, 2:651.

16. See William H. Harbaugh, *Power and Responsibility: The Life and Times of Theodore Roosevelt* (New York: Farrar, Straus and Cudahy, 1961).

17. Roosevelt was telling Walker that the latter's task was to inform the president's principal assistant, the imperious James F. Byrnes, that he was out, so far as concerned the vice-presidential nomination in 1944. Walker protested mildly, to which the president remarked that that was the way the game was played. For awkward tasks, such as dispensing bad news, the president used his assistants. If the messengers got into trouble, that was their problem, and Roosevelt more than once denied he commissioned them. This piquant point appears in drafts for Walker's unpublished autobiography, now in the Walker Papers in the Archives of the University of Notre Dame, Hesburgh Library, South Bend, Indiana.

18. "I explain the Norton episode in some detail not so much because of my personal feelings — although they were bitter at the time — but because it was a turning point in the evolution of the White House staff. The small, intimate group that had previously gathered devotedly around the President and had considered itself on familiar terms with him was never completely restored. This was not entirely a result of Norton's operations, although they delineated the change. The fact was that the office of the Presidency was becoming too big and too busy to permit continuance of the old set-up. Somewhere in Taft's administration the one-big-family atmosphere faded out, and when Woodrow Wilson became President, the times had changed and we were in a busy office that had little chance for byplay, gossip, or an occasional game of craps in the basement." Smith, *"Dear Mr. President,"* 77.

19. Ibid., 112–14.

20. Robert H. Ferrell, *Peace in Their Time: The Origins of the Kellogg-Briand Pact* (New Haven: Yale University Press, 1952), 45.

21. Robert H. Ferrell, ed., *Truman in the White House: The Diary of Eben A. Ayers* (Columbia: University of Missouri Press, 1991), 186–87. Ayers, assistant press secretary in the White House, was accustomed to having his hair cut by the White House doorman, John Mays, who told him this story.

22. Seale, *President's House*, 2:949.

23. Hearing the Republican Roosevelt's lament, the wry Elihu Root replied, "McKim was not counting on always having so decrepit a President." Ibid., 682.

24. Robert H. Ferrell, ed., *Off the Record: The Private Papers of Harry S. Truman* (New York: Harper & Row, 1980), 40.

Chapter

7

The Press,
Protesters, and Presidents

Eugene L. Roberts, Jr., and Douglas B. Ward

As the military readied its war planes during the final three days before the Gulf War in January 1991, thousands of antiwar protesters came and went in Lafayette Park, across the street from the White House. "I thought if President Bush could see people saying no, it might make him stop," said Beth Aroot of McLean, Virginia, explaining why she stood in the rain at noontime, just seven hours before the bombing began. Over at the White House, a public information staff of twenty-five fielded questions from hundreds of reporters. What was the president's mood? What were the president's plans? How was the president holding up? At a press conference on January 18, two days after the bombing of Iraq and Kuwait had begun, reporters bypassed the public information staff and posed questions directly to the president. They ranged from the solicitous ("What are your thoughts?") to the barbed ("Why is it that . . . any move for peace is considered an end run these days?"). The next day, a crowd of protesters estimated by police at twenty-five thousand paraded past the White House and through downtown Washington.[1]

This was American democracy in action, an elementary civics lesson in how the United States Constitution's First Amendment promises of free speech and a free press have come to be applied at the White House. Today, few things seem more entrenched in American democracy than citizens demonstrating in front of the White House, the press reporting from inside the mansion, and the public making up its mind about what to believe and whom to support. Approximately seventeen hundred news reporters hold White House press credentials;[2] and millions of Americans have paraded, picketed, or otherwise demonstrated for hundreds of causes in the streets, sidewalks, and parks around the White House. On just one day in 1992 — April 5 — 500,000 people marched past the mansion to support a woman's right to an abortion.[3] So accustomed are Washingtonians to demonstrations that they were not seriously ruffled in May 1992 when hundreds of demonstrators blocked traffic on the Fourteenth Street Bridge while on their way to the White House. "It's normal in D.C. I'm used to it," one stalled motorist, Robert Downing, said. "I think it's good. They're having a peaceful demonstration."[4]

With this kind of acceptance, it is difficult to imagine that the White House scene has not always been this way — a highly public setting for First Amendment activity. However, not until the twentieth century did either protesters or the press achieve the breakthroughs that make their activity seem so commonplace today. The growing power of the presidency during the administrations of Theodore Roosevelt and Woodrow Wilson produced news almost unceasingly and attracted the press like a magnet. The development of high-speed presses and other technology gave the press an enormous reach into a nation eager for news and information. Roosevelt and Wilson couldn't resist the chance to increase their power and public support. The First Amendment gave the press the right to exist, but it was the mutual need of the press and the presidency for each other that brought reporters into the White House and kept them there in a stormy but seemingly enduring marriage with the presidency.[5]

With a powerful president and a powerful press together in one building, how could the White House fail to attract demonstrators?

The nation was shocked, however, on January 9, 1917, when woman suffragists announced they were weary of waiting for their just rights and would picket the White House gates to try to persuade President Wilson to back a constitutional amendment guaranteeing women the right to vote. Calling themselves "silent sentinels," the pickets took up their positions at 9 A.M. on January 10, determined to avoid the rock throwing and raucous disturbances employed by woman suffragists in England. "Mr. President, What Will You Do For Woman Suffrage?"

A stern-faced soldier for women's rights stands at the northwest corner of the White House grounds. Before the United States entered World War I and his tolerance for dissent was reduced, President Wilson dealt fairly with suffragists. Large demonstrations at the White House now adhere to prescribed rules; groups of twenty-five and under are free to stand outside the gates and express their opinions. Courtesy of the Library of Congress.

asked one picket sign. "How Long Must Women Wait For Liberty?" que-
ried another. Although the methods were modest by today's standards,
rage spread across the country. The suffragists were accused of being
lawless, pernicious, impudent, ill-mannered, disrespectful, dangerously
radical, invaders of the president's privacy, and, in general, a threat to
the American way of life and to an orderly democratic process.[6]

"No one can imagine the socialists, prohibitionists or any other party
conceiving of a performance at once so petty and so monstrous," the
New York Times declared. "One could not imagine even the I.W.W.
[a radical labor organization] attempting it."[7] "Picketing the White
House," huffed the Philadelphia Inquirer, "is a piece of impudence that
would not be tolerated for a moment if it were done by men."[8] "A breach
of good manners," pronounced the Richmond Times Dispatch.[9] "If
everyone who wanted some particular measure or legislation undertook
to picket the White House," the New York World mused, "it would be
besieged by a mob reaching from Baltimore to Richmond."[10] "There
must be sufficient law to deal with their pernicious activities," said the
Public Ledger of Philadelphia. "If there is not, a law should be passed
forbidding them. The nation, not the President, is shamed by the acts of
these deluded campaigners."[11]

The Washington Evening Star suggested the pickets might want to
change the scene of their protest — to the Capitol. "If picketing has any
value whatever it should be undertaken at the Capitol, the scene of legislation, the place to which the suffragists must look for action," the
Star said.[12]

It seems clear that much of the nation and the press opposed the picketing, at least in part because they looked upon the White House as a
private home, rather than as an official residence that doubled as a government nerve center. The irony was that the press, worried as it was in
its editorials about the privacy of the president, now had a permanent
office inside the White House, pried as much news as possible from
visitors to the president's office, and was coming to believe its access
was embodied in the First Amendment. It does not seem to have occurred to the Star and other newspapers that by covering the White
House with steadily increasing intensity, they were making it an inevi-

table target for advocates seeking to advance their causes through publicity.

The press can be forgiven, perhaps, for its insensitivity because its access to the presidential home was relatively new. Until 1896 the White House was ignored by the press as an ongoing news center. The change came that year, as George Juergens pieced together in *News from the White House,* when Harry Godwin, the *Star*'s city editor, tried to get rid of a job seeker by suggesting he go to the White House and see if he could come up with a story for the paper. As Godwin figured it, President Grover Cleveland was so hostile to the press, the would-be reporter would fail in the assignment and never again darken the door of the *Star.* But the eager job applicant, William "Fatty" Price, all three hundred pounds of him, had a secret weapon: ignorance. He did not know he was supposed to fail, and he knew nothing about the way Washington reporting was conducted. However, he had been the editor of a small weekly in South Carolina and had gathered news for it by dropping by the local depot and interviewing the passengers that stopped in town each day. When Price arrived at the White House, he did what he had done down South: he stood outside and talked to the people who were coming and going. He got one story, then others, then a job.[13]

Other newspapers were quick to notice the *Star*'s success at the White House gates and sent their own reporters to join Fatty Price. By early 1900 there were enough reporters consistently on the streets around the White House to prompt President William McKinley to initiate daily briefings for them by his secretary. In the fall of 1901, an assassin killed McKinley. The new president was Theodore Roosevelt, who had become accustomed to dealing with reporters while he was police commissioner of New York City and, later, governor of New York State. Teddy Roosevelt seemed genuinely to like newsmen; but, sentiment aside, he recognized that his success in governing the nation hinged to some degree upon his ability to communicate to it through the press. He began briefing reporters himself, usually in casual, off-the-record get-togethers in his office. Those who irritated the president weren't invited to the presidential chats. Those who pleased him with their stories were welcomed warmly to his office. Not all the journalists were comfortable with Roosevelt and his ways, which they viewed as managing the news. Whether they liked him or not, though, they all gained from his approach to the press. The status of the White House correspondent soared, not only because Roosevelt welcomed news reporters into the White House, but because he gave them a permanent workplace.[14]

One cold, rainy day in 1902, according to press lore, Roosevelt looked out his office window and saw drenched newsmen huddling under the North Portico while waiting to interview visitors. He immediately ordered that an anteroom next to his study be set aside for a reporters' lounge and writing room. A better arrangement came a few months later. With the arrival of Roosevelt's six children, the White House became cramped, and Congress appropriated $540,000 for renovation and construction of a West Wing for offices. Roosevelt directed that a room next to his secretary's be designed and constructed especially for the press corps. It was an important step for the White House correspondents. "It conferred a sort of legitimacy on their presence," Juergens wrote in *News from the White House.* "It suggested that they were no longer there just as guests of the President; they were fulfilling a public function."[15]

Another breakthrough in press access at the White House came in 1913 when, just eleven days after his inauguration, President Woodrow Wilson convened the first White House press conference. Wilson did not feel comfortable with the sort of familiarity that existed between Teddy Roosevelt and his favorite reporters, but felt that he, too, needed the press to reach the public. He decided to see the correspondents all together in twice-a-week conferences in which he would lead off with any statements he wanted to make and then open himself to reporters' questions. Although Wilson gave up the experiment after twenty-one months, unhappy that, among other things, the press wouldn't limit its questions to the subjects he thought important, the idea of periodic exchanges between the president and the press took root.

In 1914 the reporters took their own step for permanency by forming the White House Correspondents' Association with eleven charter members and with "Fatty" Price, the man who started it all, as the founding chairman. It would deal directly with the president's operatives in matters affecting press–White House relations and would discipline members who violated ground rules the organization worked out with presidential representatives. By 1917, as the press saw it, the First Amendment had a firm foundation inside the White House. It remained to be seen whether the suffragists could successfully implant the amendment on the walkways and streets outside.[16]

Considering the foreboding on editorial pages after the suffragists announced their plans to picket, the first few months of demonstrations were surprisingly anticlimactic. Wilson and his staff initially reacted good-spiritedly. When the president's car drove past the pickets, he sometimes acknowledged them with a smile, a wave, or a salute. When what the *Star* described as a "cold, piercing wind" blew across the White House grounds on the second day of picketing, presidential aides invited the pickets into the mansion to warm themselves. The pickets said they could not accept without the permission of their leaders. The leaders responded by shortening the tours of duty for the pickets and supplying them with hot chocolate.[17]

Despite their efforts, the suffragists struggled to keep interest in the picketing alive. They held "state days" on which delegations from Maryland, Pennsylvania, New York, Virginia, and New Jersey came in turn. The White House remained calm. So did the public. Picketing dropped from the front pages. Then inside-the-paper coverage became sporadic.

The mood began to swing in April, when the United States entered World War I, and the suffragists continued their picketing, despite criticism that it was unpatriotic. Suffragists recalled that Susan B. Anthony had reluctantly cut down on her prosuffrage activities during the Civil War, only to see the vote granted at war's end to black males, but not to women.

When world leaders showed up at the White House to meet with President Wilson about war plans, the suffragists greeted them with picket signs. Arthur Balfour, leader of the British mission, called at the White House and saw suffragist banners inscribed with the precise words Wilson had used in his war message: "We shall fight for the things which we have always held nearest our hearts — for democracy, for the right of

those who submit to authority to have a voice in their own governments."[18]

On June 22 the signs greeting a delegation from the new Russian republic were more pointed. A huge banner said: "President Wilson and
Envoy [Elihu] Root are deceiving Russia when they say 'We are a Democracy, help us win the world war so that democracy may survive.' We
the women of America tell you that America is not a democracy.
Twenty million American women are denied the right to vote. President
Wilson is the chief opponent of their national enfranchisement. Help us
make this nation really free. Tell our Government it must liberate its
people before it can claim Free Russia as an ally." Anger spread through
the White House, the government, and the streets. Within twenty-four
hours, hecklers pulled down the banner three times — once with police
looking on.[19]

As tensions grew, officials of the District of Columbia police informed the pickets they would be arrested if they returned. Rows of
policemen formed outside the pickets' headquarters the next day and,
within minutes, arrested two pickets who marched to the White House.
The first pickets were released without charges. But, ultimately, ninety-
seven women spent up to six months in the Occoquan workhouse.
When they refused to eat, they were wrestled to the floor or their beds,
and tubes were shoved down their throats. Thirty women resisted so
persistently that the Wilson administration worried that some might
die. A shift in public opinion to the women's cause added to the worry.
It was the beginning of the end.[20]

On November 27 and 29, all of the pickets were released uncondition-
ally from prison. On January 9, 1918, President Wilson reversed his position on suffrage and announced he was now in favor of a constitutional
amendment. The amendment cleared Congress in the summer of 1919
and, with three-quarters of the states approving, was adopted on August
26, 1920.[21]

In winning the right for women to vote, the suffragists also established the right to picket the White House for future generations of both
sexes. More than three months after the pickets were released from
prison, the U.S. Court of Appeals for the District of Columbia ruled that

their arrests and sentences were invalid: they had been breaking no law in picketing the White House, even in wartime.[22]

The establishment of a citizen's right to picket the president did not touch off, as the suffragists' critics predicted, an immediate rush of protesters and crusaders to the White House. There was only sporadic picketing in the 1920s. Near the end of the Herbert Hoover administration in 1931, there was a flurry of demonstrations against hunger and for unemployment relief, and demonstrations by the unemployed and impoverished continued into the New Deal era of President Franklin D. Roosevelt. The most publicized of all demonstrations before World War II, ironically, never took place — the proposed march on Washington by A. Philip Randolph and other black activists. As Randolph visualized it, up to 100,000 blacks would parade past the White House along Pennsylvania Avenue to demand fair treatment in the military and a fair share of jobs in the defense industry, which was gearing up as the nation prepared for possible entry into the war. The administration grew jittery. Some critics feared chaos in Washington if black demonstrators tried to eat in the city's then-segregated restaurants or sleep in its whites-only hotels.[23]

Randolph called off the march only after President Roosevelt authorized the creation of the Fair Employment Practices Commission to help open defense jobs to blacks. The march on Washington movement, as it was called, was an important development in African-American history because it envisioned the kind of massive, nonviolent demonstrations staged by the civil rights movement in the 1960s to bring about sweeping racial change in the South.

In the decade after World War II, the tensest White House demonstration came while Julius and Ethel Rosenberg unsuccessfully appealed against execution in the electric chair for having been convicted as atom spies. Police warded off all but minor clashes by threading their way through a crowd of seven thousand, keeping death-penalty advocates separated from Rosenberg supporters.[24]

Nothing in the 1950s or in previous decades, however, quite prepared White House security forces for the 1960s. There was an explosion of issues — nuclear weapons, Fidel Castro, racial integration, the Congo, disarmament — and they all made their way to the White House. According to police counts at the time, demonstrators protested in front of the mansion on 96 days in 1960 and on 229 days in 1961. Picketing was so common in 1962 that a White House police officer observed, "It seems like it's getting to be a national habit." Reeling from all the activity, the White House police won approval in June 1962 to increase its staff from 170 to 250. In 1963 Philip Randolph's vision of a massive civil rights march on Washington came true. A dense carpet of people, estimated variously at 200,000 to 500,000, spread out from each side of the Reflecting Pool near the Washington Monument, scores of thousands of them having passed by the White House. Martin Luther King, Jr., emblazoned the day on the national memory by aiming his "I Have a Dream" speech to the crowd, the nation, Congress, and especially President John F. Kennedy. While the crowd was dispersing, King and other civil rights leaders met in the White House with President Kennedy for seventy-two minutes, urging him to press Congress for strong civil rights legislation.[25]

Later in the decade, as the United States stepped up its involvement in Vietnam, and as the civil rights movement gained momentum, the early 1960s would, in retrospect, seem almost idyllic. Although the right to demonstrate outside the White House was clearly established, civil rights and antiwar activists took their protest onto the mansion grounds and into the White House itself. The protesters posed as tourists, joined guided tours, and then broke away to participate in an array of sit-in, lie-in, and pray-in demonstrations. Outside the White House, the demonstrations grew so intense that President Richard Nixon's security officers had buses parked bumper-to-bumper on the south front of the mansion to create a massive protective barrier against the protesters.[26]

Meanwhile, inside the White House in the 1960s and 1970s, the size of the press corps soared. The growth of television contributed, as did the growing power of the presidency. As late as World War II, the president called most of the correspondents by their first names. No more. Hundreds jammed press conferences, with television becoming ever more important. In 1964 President Johnson gave approval for the three televison networks — NBC, ABC, and CBS — to build a television studio at their own expense, only sixty feet from his office, in the Fish Room — so called because President Franklin Roosevelt kept his tropical fish there. For the press, the leap forward in facilities came under President Nixon, who, despite tense battles with the press corps, gave up the White House swimming pool, three rub-down rooms, a sauna, some dog kennels, and a room for fashioning floral decorations in order to create a new double-decker press facility with twelve broadcast booths, forty writing desks, and a briefing room. Some of the reporters suspected Nixon of orchestrating the move to get them further away from his key staff members. Until then, the correspondents used the same room Teddy Roosevelt had set aside for them more than sixty years before. There was much for reporters to cover from the new facilities — the regulation of White House protests, for example.[27]

The intensity of the demonstrations, combined with the assassinations of Robert Kennedy and Martin Luther King, Jr., in 1968, spurred the growth of federal regulations governing demonstrations near the White House. Protest organizations fought back with lawsuits and appeals of arrests. Between 1971 and 1992, a series of twenty-four federal court decisions shaped the nearly five pages of U.S. Park Service regulations that now govern demonstrations at the White House and nearby parks and monuments.[28]

Today groups of up to twenty-five people may demonstrate without permits or notice to the government. Larger groups must give notice, get permits, and restrict their demonstrations to 750 people on White House sidewalks or 3,000 in Lafayette Park unless they get a special exemption from the Park Service. No camping is allowed, and use of structures and equipment other than picket signs is tightly regulated.[29]

Despite the regulations, demonstrators keep flocking to the White House. Government officials years ago gave up tracking demonstrations by protest days as they did in the 1950s and early 1960s. One small group of nuclear disarmament activists has been demonstrating daily for almost ten years. In the first nine months of 1992, 128 permits were issued to groups of more than twenty-five.[30]

By and large, the courts have been sympathetic to regulations designed to protect the president's life and to anti-camping rules aimed at keeping public areas sanitary. The courts have been cool, though, to

Opponents of the use of American armed forces to free Kuwait from Iraq's occupation in 1991 protest in the park opposite the front of the White House. Courtesy of the *Philadelphia Inquirer*.

rules designed for other reasons, including protecting the president's sleep.

During the demonstrations against the Gulf War, the protesters in Lafayette Park chanted, waved signs, and beat a drum so loudly and so incessantly that President Bush complained it kept him awake at night. U.S. Park Service police arrested a drummer and charged her with violating the "decibel levels" regulation aimed at preserving the tranquillity of federal parks. A three-judge panel of the U.S. Court of Appeals overturned the conviction. In a ruling that would have delighted the suffragist pickets, the court said the Park Service could not expect to regulate the area around the White House like a normal park. The reason was simple. The area, the court said, has become "a primary assembly point for First Amendment activity."[31]

NOTES

1. See, for instance, Alessandra Stanley, "As War Looms: Marches and Vigils, Talk and Fear," *New York Times*, January 15, 1991, A15; Alessandra Stanley, "Personal Steps in March of History," *New York Times*, January 16, 1991, A1; James Barron, "A Tense Wait," *New York Times*, January 17, 1991, A1; "Excerpts from the Remarks by Bush on Israel and the War Against Iraq," *New York Times*, January 19, 1991, A12; "Across America, Demonstrators Take Sides in Persian Gulf War," photo caption, *New York Times*, January 20, 1991, A18; Peter Applebome, "News from Front Blunts Protest," *New York Times*, January 21, 1991, A12.

2. Laura Mellillo, deputy White House press secretary, interview with author, October 1, 1992.

3. The crowd estimate was made by District of Columbia and U.S. Park Service Police. See, for instance, Karen Schneider, "Abortion-rights rally in D.C. draws 500,000," *Philadelphia Inquirer*, April 6, 1992, A1; and Christine Spolar, "Abortion-Rights Rally Draws Half a Million Marchers," *Washington Post*, April 6, 1992, A1.

4. The protests were spurred by a California jury's acquittal of white police officers who beat Rodney King, a black man, in Los Angeles. See Matt Neufeld, "Bush releases $600 million for L.A.; Protesters Block 14th Street Bridge," *Washington Times*, May 5, 1992, LEXIS/NEXIS.

5. See, for instance, George Juergens, *News from the White House* (Chicago: University of Chicago Press, 1981); Donald A. Ritchie, *Press Gallery* (Cambridge: Harvard University Press, 1991), and John Tebbel and Sarah Miles Watt,

The Press and the Presidency: From George Washington to Ronald Reagan (New York: Oxford University Press, 1985).

6. See, for instance, Aileen S. Kraditor, *The Ideas of the Woman Suffrage Movement, 1890–1920* (New York: Columbia University Press, 1965), 219–48; Inez Hayes Irwin, *The Story of Alice Paul and the National Woman's Party* (Fairfax, Va.: Denlinger's Publishers, 1977), 198–218; Doris Stevens, *Jailed for Freedom* (New York: Boni and Liveright, 1920), 66–79; and Elizabeth Frost and Kathryn Cullen-DuPont, *Women's Suffrage in America: An Eyewitness History* (New York: Facts on File, 1992), 315–36.

7. "Silent, Silly and Offensive," *New York Times*, January 11, 1917, 14.

8. "Editorial Comment," *Philadelphia Inquirer*, January 12, 1917, 8.

9. See "Picketing the White House," *Washington Evening Star*, January 14, 1917, 4, for comment from several newspapers.

10. Ibid.

11. Ibid.

12. "Why 'Picket' the White House?" *Washington Evening Star*, January 12, 1917, 6.

13. Juergens, *News from the White House*; also see Rodger Streitmatter, "William W. Price: First White House Correspondent and Emblem of an Era," *Journalism History* 16 (Summer 1989): 32–41.

14. Juergens, *News from the White House*; Ritchie, *Press Gallery*.

15. Juergens, *News from the White House*, 16.

16. Juergens, *News from the White House*; Ritchie, *Press Gallery*; Tebbel and Watt, *The Press and the Presidency*.

17. "Cold Drives Off Suffrage Pickets," *Washington Evening Star*, January 11, 1917, 3; "Suffrage Parade Plan Abandoned," *Washington Evening Star*, January 12, 1917, 2; "Freezing Suffrage 'Sentinels' Ignore Invitation by Wilson to Come Inside and Get Warm," *Washington Post*, January 12, 1917, 5; "Shivering Pickets Salute Wilson As He Smiles Upon Suffrage Squad," *Washington Post*, January 13, 1917, 2; also see William Seale, *The President's House: A History* (Washington: White House Historical Association, 1986), 805.

18. Stevens, *Jailed for Freedom*, 84; Irwin, *Story of Alice Paul*, 214.

19. Stevens, *Jailed for Freedom*, 92.

20. Stevens, *Jailed for Freedom*, Part III, and Irwin, *Story of Alice Paul*, 198–315, provide good overviews.

21. Ibid.

22. Irwin, *Story of Alice Paul*, 267–68.

23. The *Bulletin* Collection, Urban Archives, Temple University, provides a good overview of some of the major protests over the years. See specifically the file titled "Washington, D.C. — White House — Picketing and Intruders." The morgue at the *Philadelphia Inquirer* also has many clippings about protests in files headed "White House, General," in various periods. For information about

Randolph, see Taylor Branch, *Parting the Waters* (New York: Simon & Schuster, 1988), 846–87; and Paula F. Pfeffer, *A. Philip Randolph: Pioneer of the Civil Rights Movement* (Baton Rouge: Louisiana State University Press, 1990), 45–88.

24. See "Pickets, March for Rosenbergs," June 15, 1953, and "Rosenberg Pickets Kept Apart at White House," February 23, 1953, *Bulletin* Collection, Temple University; and Alvin Spivak, "Picket lines appear so often outside the White House it's getting to be a national habit," June 2, 1962, *Inquirer* clip file, "White House — General — 1962."

25. The *Bulletin* and *Inquirer* clip files again provide good overviews; for the number of protests, see Alvin Spivak, "Picket lines appear so often outside the White House it's getting to be a national habit," June 2, 1962, *Inquirer* clip file, "White House — General — 1962"; for an overview of the March on Washington, see Pfeffer, *A. Philip Randolph*.

26. See, for instance, various articles from the *Bulletin* Collection, files labeled "Washington, D.C. — White House — Picketing and Intruders": Holmes Alexander, "Justice Department Would Seal Off White House," April 7, 1970; "White House Invasion," March 14, 1965; Robert Roth, "Sit-Ins Precipitated 'Crisis,' " March 14, 1965; Anthony Day, "Johnson Bars Further Lie-Ins in White House," March 12, 1965; "36 Arrested Sitting Outside White House," March 13, 1965; and "Sitters Seized in Driveway at White House," April 20, 1965; and various articles from the *Inquirer* clip files labeled "White House — General": William J. Eaton, "U.S. Officials Move to Limit Gatherings Around White House," June 15, 1970; William Vance, "White House Police Arrest 3 Phila. Youth," May 20, 1972; and "2 More Held at White House," July 13, 1973. Also see Richard D. Lyons, "White House Once a Place That 'Belonged' to Public," *New York Times*, May 9, 1970, 9.

27. See, for instance, Luther A. Huston, "Nixon Puts Newsmen in Lap of Luxury," *Editor & Publisher*, April 18, 1970, 18; and Saul Kohler, "Old Swimming Pool to be Press Room," *Philadelphia Inquirer*, October 22, 1969, and Richard K. Doan, "TV Million for Fish Room," *New York Herald-Tribune*, January 28, 1964, *Inquirer* clip files, "White House — General"; Peter Braestrup, former reporter for the *New York Herald-Tribune*, the *New York Times*, and the *Washington Post*, interview with author, October 9, 1992; also see Tebbel and Watt, *The Press and the Presidency*.

28. Randolph Myers, attorney, National Capital Parks Branch, Office of the Solicitor, U.S. Department of the Interior, interview with author, October 9, 1992.

29. *Code of Federal Regulations, Parks Forest and Public Property* 36 (July 1, 1992): 121–29.

30. Rachel Mullally, Office of Public Events, U.S. Park Service, interview with author, October 9, 1992.

31. See Pam Weisz, "In Lafayette Park, freedom to be loud; But across the

street, arrests for NOW," *Washington Times*, July 1, 1992, A1; "U.S. can't en-force tranquility at White House park: Judges," *Chicago Tribune*, July 1, 1992, 4; and *Washington Post*, "Noise Rule Struck Down," July 2, 1992, D3; LEXIS/NEXIS.

The President and the Media:

An Adversarial
but Helpful Relationship

George E. Reedy

The systematic relations of the modern White House with the national and the international news media actually began with the administration of Franklin Delano Roosevelt. That statement, however, is not merely a basis for a chronology. Its true significance lies in the light it sheds on the political, social, and economic revolution that changed American life irrevocably in the fourth decade of the twentieth century. A by-product of that revolution was the establishment of the presidency as a focal point for the full-time attention of our citizens when discussing the important issues before our society.

It may surprise most Americans ten or more years younger than I to learn that this was not the case for most of our history. Wartime presidents such as Lincoln and Wilson were obviously the center of all eyes. A colorful character, such as Theodore Roosevelt, received considerable press play. Thomas Jefferson became widely known while president for the Louisiana Purchase.

Our studies of history in elementary and high school obscure the social reality. The Founding Fathers — men such as Washington, the two Adamses, and Monroe — have taken on a semimythical aura similar to that which enveloped Achilles and Ajax in the *Iliad*. It is easy to think that the whole nation watched them in awe. But the majority of Americans, even after the adoption of the Constitution, still regarded themselves as Virginians or New Yorkers or Rhode Islanders first and citizens of the United States second. Those who had advocated a strong central government did so largely to attain some unity in dealing with other nations and to find means of stabilizing the currency. Many of our people had no real interest in such questions, and some wanted to cut off all relations with other nations and preferred an unstable currency. The press of that period consisted of partisan newspapers that did mention presidents often. But the readership was small and did not reflect the thinking of most Americans.

Before the New Deal, when Americans needed government help, they looked for it in their city, town, or county administrations. Except in wartime, the groups most interested in Washington and the White House were lobbyists seeking railroad land grants or the opening of public lands to settlement. In the more sparsely populated regions, state governments had considerable influence, but the major issue was protection against lawbreakers. Under such circumstances, the nation's press paid little attention to the White House, although presidential campaigns might receive some attention when a candidate came into home territory.

One of my experiences from the 1920s illustrates this point. My father took my mother and me on a driving vacation in the East. Although I could not have been more than eight years old, I was fairly sophisticated about journalism, as my father was a police reporter for the *Chicago Tribune* (in an era when the battles between gangs was the major topic of editorial attention). When we reached Washington, he contacted the *Tribune*'s two correspondents — John and Genevieve Forbes Herrick. I listened in fascination as they talked about their work in the nation's capital.

The most important point that emerged from those discussions was that the Herricks focused their activities on the Illinois congressional delegation. They made no systematic effort whatsoever to cover the president or the White House, and when the president was included in something they wrote, the source of the story would be either an Illinois congressman or a legislative hearing in which Illinois was involved. The *Tribune* relied on the wire services (Associated Press and United Press International) for any other type of presidential story that the editors thought had to be printed. To place this point in context, it should be noted that the presidents of the 1920s were ideologically in full step with the *Chicago Tribune* — an ultra-conservative, Republican newspaper.

Almost as important was my discovery that we really had a live, breathing president. This came about because, on a public tour of the White House, my mother was charmed by a picture of Grace Coolidge in a red dress alongside a white collie dog. (The picture still hangs in the same place.) I returned to Chicago bursting with the information that Warren G. Harding — who was fairly well known because of the Teapot Dome scandal — had been succeeded by a man named Calvin Coolidge. My playmates in school could not have cared less. They had no idea of the nature of the presidency or what the president did to earn his pay. But all of them could name the leader of our ward, their precinct captain, their block captain, and, of course, their alderman and their mayor. They could also outline their functions. To them, these men were real.

The public consciousness of the presidency began to change with the last chief executive of that era — Herbert Hoover. The depression that hit in 1929 was traumatic. Factory after factory shut down, and more and more people were thrown out on the street. Tens of thousands of homeless men slept in the parks every night, and Chicago's Loop district — the center of the city's commercial life — became filled with World War I veterans peddling apples at a nickel apiece under a special license. The local governments could not cope with the situation, and eyes began to turn to Washington. To many it seemed that Hoover could do nothing other than issue a few fatuous statements that "the foundations of the economy are sound." In fact, he sent Congress some bills to combat the depression, and a few actually passed. Most of his bills, however, were turned down by a Congress that had come under the control of the Democrats. The press coverage of Washington mushroomed, but it did so to make Hoover a deep-dyed villain in the public eye. Ironically, the man who did so much to establish the White House in the American consciousness was known popularly for inaction rather than action.

In 1932 Franklin D. Roosevelt's election was a foregone conclusion, and, with his inauguration, Washington became a hotbed of activity. He declared a "bank holiday" to stop runs on deposits that were bankrupting institutions everywhere. Congress received a flood of major bills, which it began approving at a rate of almost one a day. Most important for our purposes, Roosevelt announced that he would hold two press conferences a week, at which he would appear and respond to any questions. One conference was held on Wednesday mornings for the afternoon press and one on Friday afternoons for the morning press. (These were later moved back one day.) He also designated a specific assistant — Steve Early — to handle press queries on a full-time basis.

This was not the first time that presidents had opened up contacts with the media. Theodore Roosevelt was famous for having some "trained seal" reporters who received exclusive stories in return for writing them the Rooseveltian way. Woodrow Wilson had tried holding free-style press conferences, but his personality was too abrasive, and he spent so much time fighting with journalists that the whole thing was abandoned. Herbert Hoover would, at times, appear before reporters and read written answers to written questions. These developments could be interpreted as evidence that social and economic conditions were changing and that a large, capitalistic democracy needed continuing dialogue with its leaders. Wilson, in particular, indicated that he appreciated the need. But it took a dramatic event and a dramatic personality to respond.

Franklin Delano Roosevelt's blueprint for dealing with the press was far-reaching. The weekly press conference led to the establishment of a permanent White House beat for the wire services and such leading newspapers as the *New York Times* and the *Washington Star*. The conferences themselves were very satisfying to the correspondents involved. I covered a few of them (not as a regular but as a congressional correspondent, called in when a major proposal had been sent to Congress). There was a genuine warmth in the sight of ten or so reporters standing around Roosevelt's desk with everyone speaking informally. A reporter who did not like an answer was free to come in with a follow-up question. In addition, the "regulars" traveled on the same train with FDR when he went out of town.

There were certain inhibitions in White House coverage. Quotation marks could not be put around anything the president said without specific authorization. But what he said could be presented verbatim. The only real purpose of the inhibition was to enable the president to blame the press if something he supposedly said got him into trouble. Reporters did not mind this; they had developed broad shoulders. In addition, no picture could be taken which would reveal the extent of the president's paralysis. The photographers were also perfectly willing to go along with this rule because FDR recognized their needs and helped them whenever he could.

The regular press conferences did not exhaust the steps taken by the president to open up continuing contact with the American people. On March 12 — eight days after his inauguration — he spoke to the country on a nationwide radio hookup in what he called a "fireside chat." It was intended to be reassuring and stressed the theme that Americans had "nothing to fear but fear itself." Later, when he thought that a press owned by Republican publishers and managed by Republican editors had turned against him, he used the "fireside chat" technique to go over the heads of the newspaper owners. Television did not exist to any practical extent at the time, or he certainly would have used that medium also.

One other development should be noted here. Mrs. Roosevelt held press conferences that she forbade any males to attend. Basically, she was trying to brighten journalistic prospects for women, who, in the early thirties, were limited almost entirely to producing newspaper articles on cooking, dress styles, and child care. It was an astute move on her part, as she made news for the front pages of any newspaper. Editors were forced either to hire women or at least to enter into contract relationships with women to cover the conference.

The fundamentals of publicizing the White House were laid down by these moves. There were sweeping changes ahead, but they largely involved the application of new technologies to these principles. The principles that remained the same were regulated, but reasonably free, press contacts with the president; the concept that the president had an obligation to submit to public questioning; and the president's use of direct channels to appeal to the public when he thought he was receiving unfair treatment.

Over the years a combination of technology and worldwide change ended the informal charm of the early FDR conferences. World War II brought about an expansion of the numbers of journalists covering the White House, and the cold war expanded their numbers even further. Follow-up questions became virtually impossible, and the large attendance gave the president forms of control that Roosevelt did not possess or seek. Radio news in the form of short, quick bulletins became standard — a development that led presidential advisers to seek punch lines for his appearances.

Television edged its way into the picture during the Eisenhower administration. Press Secretary James Hagerty prepared a format in which the conferences were filmed but not released for public use until they had been checked. The people covering the White House with whom I talked during that period did not complain about Hagerty's editing. He usually let it go through as filmed, and when he eliminated anything, it was normally because of grammar. It was only a step from the filming to the live TV conferences launched by John F. Kennedy. He was quick-witted and had an engaging TV personality. For him the experiment was a success, however much later presidents may have regretted it. Today the press conference is a creature of television, with newspaper reporters relegated to the status of analysts.

The forms of White House control over the media that have emerged from the combination of increasing numbers of reporters, the application of technology, and the accumulation of presidential experience are worth some discussion. Most presidents would deny that such forms exist or that they bar the public from important knowledge of the nation's business. Nevertheless, these forms do suggest the possibilities of a type of control over a mass society that would not be easily identifiable.

The first, and most important, of the forms of presidential control is the awesome majesty of the presidency itself when displayed in the proper setting. There is a tremendous difference between a friendly, smiling man seated at a desk surrounded by about ten people and a man standing on a platform behind the Great Seal of the President addressing a crowd that can run to 150 (maybe more) people. The first situation is one that promotes banter, cross-questions, occasional flare-ups of anger, and a thorough probing of points. The second is one that makes the audience feel like humble petitioners, grateful to the lord of the castle.

President Franklin D. Roosevelt's famous "fireside chats" were conducted from the Diplomatic Reception Room of the White House. Roosevelt's use of radio foreshadowed later presidents' televised speeches and press conferences. Harris & Ewing.

An occasional reporter — Dan Rather at a Nixon press conference, for example — may lose his or her temper and flare back at the president. But that is rare. After all, the man who is the center of attention is not only the president of the United States; he is the United States and he is speaking from what is close to a shrine. To be disrespectful to him is the equivalent of blowing one's nose in the American flag.

This situation is reinforced by the fact that the American people are watching the performance. Of course, this means a considerable amount of ego gratification for reporters who realize they are the center of all eyes. This promotes a desire to look good rather than to be sharp and nasty.

Second, the modern press conference permits the president to choose which reporters will be allowed to ask questions. By binding custom, he must allow the wire service men and women to open the session. They, after all, are regulars who must live with him full-time, and, while they will ask the necessary questions, they are going to be as moderate in tone as possible. After they have finished, asking a question requires presidential recognition, and there is virtually no opportunity for a fol-low-up if a response is unsatisfactory. For a strong personality, the situation is made to order.

Reporters who cover the White House full-time are also aware that the president has rewards he can pass out on an exclusive basis to jour-nalists who play ball. These arise out of his absolute control over a type of news that can make or break some correspondents — his own private life and personality. Things that are very trivial for every other govern-ment official can fill whole columns when they concern the chief exec-utive. The press is absolutely indifferent to the inner lives of other dig-nitaries unless they reach the point of open and notorious scandal. But extraordinary space will be devoted to personal mannerisms of the man in the Oval Office.

As press secretary I found myself agape with wonderment at the num-ber of column inches produced concerning the fact that Lyndon B. John-son had to have a freshly opened bottle of soda every time he took a drink of Scotch. Richard M. Nixon's predilection for cottage cheese and catsup together became a national byword. Even more important is the ability of the president to pass out to favored news reporters intimate

In a televised press conference President Lyndon B. Johnson announces plans for a manned orbiting space laboratory. Through such meetings twentieth-century presidents have been able to enhance the power of their office, focus public attention on selected programs, and effect press coverage of their administrations. Courtesy of the White House Historical Association.

pictures of his family life taken by a White House photographer. No journalist is going to alter the news itself for such tidbits. But their existence and possible use foster a respect that is not always in keeping with an aggressive search for news.

A further power of the president is his ability to set the tone of the press conference with his opening statement. Lyndon Johnson, for example, could defuse an especially explosive session by ordering the Defense Department to declassify some new weapon that at least sounded like an omnipotent instrument with which to threaten the Soviet Union. The breakup of the Soviet empire has put an end to the use of military hardware to create a diversion. But a search for substitutes should turn up something sooner or later.

Then there is the tactic of the planted question. Someone can always be found who will present a "stooge" query and give the president the opportunity to filibuster. He does not need to fill much time, as there is a tendency for television requirements to set the limits of the conference. Generally speaking, conferences last about half an hour.

In recent years another development has supplied a form of presidential control. It is the presence in the White House of television facilities that can be used on very short notice. This means that the president can make dramatic announcements on new topics about which the journalists are not really prepared to question him. Then, when he gets requests later for a full-blown press conference, he can claim that it is unreasonable to expect him to hold one when he has already appeared before the press on so many occasions. It is possible that the type of conference that became familiar during the Kennedy-Johnson-Nixon era may disappear altogether.

Finally, the president has the support provided by his press secretary. This person can provide the president advance warning of journalistic storms and help him handle them. The press secretary does not have to answer questions off the top of his head. When confronted with a really tough query, he can always respond that he must check it out. Furthermore, if an answer is going to hurt, he is somewhat removed from the president, and the political impact is thus somewhat softened.

The position of press secretary deserves deeper investigation than it has been given. There is a widespread misperception — shared by most presidents and even some press secretaries of the past — that it is basically a public relations job. Naturally, the person who holds it is going to recommend the chief executive highly. But there is an overriding limitation on what can be done that takes the press office out of the area of normal PR activity. This is the necessity for the press secretary to be believable. Fundamentally, he is the president's spokesman and his yea must be yea and his nay must be nay. He need be caught in a fib only once for his value as the presidential spokesman to go down the drain. Of course, he can give the president advice on public relations. And, of course, if the president is going to play games, the press secretary must repeat what he says. But it must be clear that he is faithfully reporting the president.

If the president is somewhat naive about the press (and most of them are; political and journalistic temperaments are quite dissimilar), it is possible for the press secretary to publicize himself. He can explain privately to the press that he is working feverishly to get facts for them, and then explain privately to the president that he is defending him against the press. This is an unusual situation which does not occur often. As a general rule, the press secretary is so tied up making the arrangements for press coverage of the president that he does not have the time to play games.

However, it has become increasingly clear in recent years that there is a need for a legitimate type of public relations practitioner in the White House. The various political, economic, and social organizations that once played such an important role in "selling" the president and in the public dialogue have lapsed into desuetude. Messages to our fellow Americans today must go through impersonal channels of communications, which have their own timing and their own rhythms. Statements that would be perfectly innocent when made face-to-face can be politically disastrous when filtered through the mass media. The art of public relations has changed from the Ivy Lee "stunt" variety, intended only to attract attention. It now requires the expertise to shape statements so they come to the audience in the intended form.

One must know the news cycles — the times that the media are eager for copy and the times when they are not very receptive. For example, unless it is a real blockbuster, a story released on Saturday afternoon will blush unseen on the desert air. The same story released on a Sunday will probably be blown out of all proportion. The communicator must also take into account the tendency of television to make a part look like a whole. (In 1972, the cameras created the illusion of a major boom for Ted Kennedy at the Democratic National Convention simply by interviewing a delegate who wanted to nominate him. The people around him realized he was on television and stood around him to wave at friends and relatives at home. On camera, they had the appearance of cheering masses.) One must also know which branches of the media are best for the presentation of ideas and which offer the best outlets for personality profiles and human interest stories.

A set of fortuitous circumstances has established in the White House the post of director of communications, which is slowly acquiring that knowledge. It is generally believed in Washington that President Nixon created the job to solve a political problem. He was deeply indebted to Herb Klein, who was a newspaperman expected by everyone to be his press secretary. But key members of his staff wanted another man with whom they had worked before. The office of the director of communications enabled Nixon to give both candidates for the position of press secretary suitable rewards.

How the director of communications has actually functioned is not at all clear, but the position has been held by some very able people. Herb Klein was followed by such men as Gerry Rafshoon, David Gergen, and Pat Buchanan. Late in the Bush administration it was held by Margaret Tutwiler, the former State Department spokeswoman who moved over to the White House with Secretary of State James Baker. She seemed to have the temperament needed to practice public relations in the modern sense.

There is nothing improper in the concept of an office whose job is to advance and explain the thinking of the president — as long as the office bears the proper label. Whatever problem exists is not in the exercise of the function itself but in the extremely negative reaction of the American people to the word "propaganda." This does not have the same pejorative connotation in most languages that it has in English. Latin Americans, for example, use the word (spelled the same way) to identify advertising. Any persuasive effort is a "propaganda" effort.

Presidents are handicapped if they lack an assistant of high rank who can mingle with reporters and public leaders on an informal basis and speak quietly without having every word taken as an official pronouncement of United States policy. The president cannot do this himself because every word he speaks is taken by the listeners as a national commitment. The same consideration affects the activities of the press secretary, who is his official spokesman. To deprive the White House of the benefit of relaxed conversation with outside forces is to leave the president blind to the political realities of his era.

At one time this function was handled by Democratic and Republican political organizations. Franklin D. Roosevelt, a political genius if one ever lived in this century, was well aware of the need. He leaned in part on the Irish political machines, which were still functioning when he entered the White House. Two of his strong allies were Ed Kelly of Chicago and Ed Flynn of the Bronx — organization politicians who exercised real power. Such men no longer exist. The environment that created them has vanished. The political organizations of the modern world are "cause" groups such as the National Association for the Advancement of Colored People, the National Organization for Women, and the Sierra Club. In a metaphorical sense, a president talking to their leaders is walking on low-calcium eggshells. The time is ripe to accept the need for an informal spokesperson who can argue for the president, and the instrument for such an official is at hand.

The publicization of the White House has developed along with the importance of that institution to our nation and the evolving technology of a mass society. As we have become a stronger, more centralized society, the necessity for types of communication that are impersonal and mechanical — but still meaningful — has become more urgent. The response at first was tentative and experimental. But in the 1990s, the relations of the White House with the mass media — which means with the public — have become more systematic. It is now taken for granted that we will hear from the White House almost every day of the year.

Does White House expertise in comunications pose a danger? Obviously, it is something that must be watched. But there is a saving grace that makes it unlikely that the communications power can ever be translated into dictatorial power. This power must be wielded by a hu-

man being responsive to political reality. Political reality requires that
the president still compete with the legislative and judicial branches of
our government and do so while offering the American people the type
of leadership they seek.

The bottom line is a simple one. The White House is the symbol of
the nation, its occupant *is* the nation during the years that he lives in it,
and it is important for the American people to have clear channels
through which they can view the presidency.

NOTE

George Reedy has written extensively on the presidency. *The Twilight of the
Presidency* (New York: World Publishing Company, 1970) was updated as *The
Twilight of the Presidency: From Johnson to Reagan* (New York: New American
Library, 1987). He has also published *The Presidency in Flux* (New York: Colum-
bia University Press, 1973). More of his thoughts appear in *Three Press Secretar-
ies on the Presidency and the Press: Jody Powell, George Reedy, Jerry terHorst,*
ed. Kenneth W. Thompson (Lanham, Md.: University Press of America, 1983).
Good accounts of presidential-press relations are George Juergens, *News from
the White House: The Presidential-Press Relationship in the Progressive Era*
(Chicago: University of Chicago Press, 1981); George C. Edwards, *The Public
Presidency: The Pursuit of Popular Support* (New York: St. Martin's Press, 1983);
John Tebbel and Sarah Miles Watt, *The Press and the Presidency: From George
Washington to Ronald Reagan* (New York: Oxford University Press, 1985); Robert E. Denton, Jr., and Dan F. Hahn, *Presidential Communication: Description
and Analysis* (New York: Praeger, 1986). Donald A. Ritchie, *Press Gallery: Congress and Washington Correspondents* (Cambridge: Harvard University Press,
1991), also has useful material on the presidency.

Chapter

Using the White House to Further Political Agendas

Edwin M. Yoder, Jr.

The political uses of the White House are obvious at one level, perhaps less so at another. Terms like "Rose Garden strategy," "West Wing," and "Oval Office" are now in everyday use. Every viewer of the evening news has a visual impression of the press briefing room with its familiar rostrum adorned with the presidential seal. Millions have, by various means, viewed presidents and their staffs at work and play, and all these images ultimately advance presidential political agendas.

That much would seem obvious. Historically, the story is more complex. I shall try to sort it out in two parts. I begin with a bit of historical perspective, for the most part impressionistic. Then I relate a few of my own experiences as a journalist visiting the President's House. I am speaking, mostly, of the physical, not the institutional, White House. The latter, now evolved from a small staff with a "passion for anonymity" to a cast of hundreds, is a subject in itself.

In her valuable history of Washington, Constance McLaughlin Green relates that during Theodore Roosevelt's time, "touches of small-town simplicity remained" at the White House.

> Small Roosevelts and velocipedes took over the upper floors of the house while on Saturday morning their father shook hands with visitors touring the mansion, his famous grin particularly warm for mothers trailed by a string of children. Almost any well-mannered white person could still wangle an invitation to a White House reception. . . . In fact, the character of official entertaining changed very little before 1913, although Mrs. Taft

155

put footmen into livery . . . in order to spare visitors the discomfort of mistaking a fellow guest for a servant.[1]

In that more innocent era, the White House must have struck visitors as more domestic than political or promotional. The Executive Mansion could not be mobilized to project presidential agendas before the rise of the modern mass media, or, indeed, before there were such agendas. For complex institutional reasons, the programmatic presidency, as one might call it, is actually a twentieth-century phenomenon.[2]

As George Will reminds us in his recent book, *Restoration*, among the articles of impeachment brought against Andrew Johnson (many of them politically and constitutionally frivolous in any case), there was the strange charge — strange to our ears, anyway — that "unmindful of the high duties of his office and the dignity and propriety thereof . . . he did . . . make and deliver with a loud voice orations intemperate, inflammatory and scandalous harangues . . . which said utterances . . . highly censurable in any, are particularly indecent and unbecoming in the Chief Magistrate of the United States."[3] Johnson's notorious "swing around the circle" in the congressional election of 1866 — an aggressive bit of electioneering against congressmen and senators who contested his views on Reconstruction — was deemed so unusual as to be nearly unnatural and certainly undignified. This was apparently not only because of Johnson's blunt language. The exercise had explosively counterproductive results.[4] There was a feeling that it did not comport with the dignity of the presidency. The custom of front-porch campaigning — even of the fiction that it was unseemly to seek the presidential office for oneself — died hard. It apparently survived the Civil War era and persisted in some forms late into the nineteenth century.[5] Obviously, a presidency so conceived would not have included the use of the Executive Mansion to promote a political agenda.

When did this change? While one might argue over the exact date, the emergence of the programmatic presidency, the presidency with an agenda in the current sense, is of recent vintage. Elements of it emerged in Theodore Roosevelt's time, although, as we have seen, his White House, as pictured by Constance Green, was quite domestic. There were elements of the programmatic presidency in the aims of his great rival,

President Franklin D. Roosevelt utilized visits by dignitaries such as British Prime Minister Winston Churchill to the White House during World War II to send messages about our confidence to Americans, our allies, and our enemies. Courtesy of Franklin D. Roosevelt Library.

Woodrow Wilson. Perhaps there was a bit of it in the twenties. But it was not, I would suggest, until the advent of Franklin D. Roosevelt's "fireside chats" in 1933 that the physical White House clearly became associated with a presidential political agenda.

Even then, we have it on excellent firsthand authority that the White House retained the ambience of a private dwelling. In his recent memoirs, the journalist Joseph W. Alsop has left a vivid picture of the Sunday evening drop-ins held, without servants or staff, by his cousins Franklin and Eleanor Roosevelt. The highlight (or low point, from the position of a gourmet like Alsop) was the ritual preparation of gooey scrambled eggs by Mrs. Roosevelt in an ancient family chafing dish. "An old-fashioned gentleman's house": that was the mood of the Executive Mansion as Alsop, no mean observer of architecture, viewed it in the mid-1930s. "Scrambled eggs," Alsop adds, "are not an easy dish to cook in such a manner that hungry men turn away in discouragement, yet even I found the eggs Cousin Eleanor made . . . for Sunday suppers discouraging."[6]

Although he would be regarded by most historians as the founder of the modern programmatic presidency, even Franklin D. Roosevelt kept what was an intimate and familial White House. His regular news conferences took place in informal groupings around the president's desk in the Oval Office — as did President Truman's. Alsop again: "Newspaper work in the Washington I knew before the war had not vastly advanced from the early stage best represented by the successful enterprise of the lady reporter who got an interview with John Quincy Adams by the simple expedient of catching the president in the Potomac River during one of his habitual before-breakfast swims and sitting on his clothes on the bank until he promised to talk to her."[7] A few years later, the Trumans vacated the White House for much of their time, pending the controversial remodeling. In those pre-electronic days, few specific instances come to mind in which the White House was put to visual use as a symbol of presidential political authority and purpose.

Thus we come, in this brief survey, to Dwight D. Eisenhower and the year 1953. Eisenhower was the first president of the television age to occupy the White House full-time. Not surprisingly, television rapidly became a significant mediator of the presidential agenda. For the first time, the American public grew accustomed to a scene that is now so common as to be taken for granted — a president discussing his program against a White House backdrop. The intimacy of the FDR-Truman news conference vanished. Eisenhower was the first president actually to be coached on his visual presentation — by the actor Robert Montgomery, if memory serves. The advent of a Hollywood coach, even on a part-time basis, was concealed at first as a sort of guilty secret.[8] Many found it shocking that a presidential agenda might now be merchandised as if it were soap or autos. What we now take for granted seemed strange then — the use of the White House and its superb surroundings as props in a marketing technique. James Hagerty, the former *New York Times* reporter and Eisenhower's astute press secretary, instituted other breakthroughs. From 1953 onward, radio tapes were made available of presidential news conferences. Beginning in 1955, television cameras were admitted. The videotapes could not be simultaneously broadcast. They were retained for vetting and editing before being released. Nineteen fifty-five was, then, a pivotal year in the use of the physical White House to promote presidential political agendas. But, once admitted, the new technology soon got the upper hand.

It was John F. Kennedy who, on January 25, 1961, after only five days in office, waived the more cautious Hagerty approach to the televised news conference and turned it into a live performance — what Charles Roberts of *Newsweek* has called "a dinner-time prime-time show." No fewer than 418 reporters (breaking the previous record by about a hundred, according to Roberts's calculation) crowded into the new State Department auditorium. The viewing audience was estimated at 60 million. To be sure, this was not the White House; but the show would return there shortly and in other ways. Kennedy really opened the White House to television, and he took advantage of other forms of photography as well. In David McCullough's splendid PBS series, "The Kennedys," Pierre Salinger, Kennedy's press secretary, recalled that the president would mischievously seize upon Jacqueline Kennedy's absences to advance his visual agenda. She very carefully guarded the children's privacy. The president would instruct Salinger to bring the photographers in to catch the fetching children at play. For her part Mrs. Kennedy conducted a memorable guided tour of the refurbished and redecorated White House, a far cry from Thomas Jefferson's mockingbird and carpet slippers.[9] This again heightened public consciousness of the mansion as a potent political symbol. From there it was off to the races.

Lyndon Johnson was perhaps a sort of sport, a mutant, in the linear development of the White House as a visual symbol of presidential agendas. He was not very good on television. His voice could be tiresome, and, by most assessments, his manner rapidly satiated the audience. Johnson was nonetheless obsessed with television and may well hold the presidential record for the consumption of televised news. He understood its power and tried to bend it to his purposes. We recall how Johnson would wander about the White House turning off the lights, a symbol of economy for which he got good marks. But he shocked city-bred reporters by lifting his beagles, Him and Her, by the ears. There came a day when he showed the cameras his surgical scars — an image soon immortalized, to his detriment, by a savage David Levine cartoon in which the scar turned into Vietnam. In Johnson's time we settled down not merely to a visual White House whose every image seemed in some way more political than domestic, but also to a dramatized White House. The apparatuses of power and authority later to be termed "imperial" began to multiply: the Marine helicopters on the South Lawn, the breathless sense of busy people hastening about, Rose Garden bill signings. All of this intensified in the Nixon years, reaching a brief and mercifully temporary ne plus ultra with the strange Graustarkian uniforms for White House guards. For the first time, there was an Office of Telecommunications Policy, commanded by a genuine doctor of communication.

President Carter, by contrast, calculatedly de-imperialized the White House. From the outset he made a self-conscious attempt to suggest to the American people that the White House had again become the dwelling of the First Citizen. He even carried his own suit bag and greeted the public in blue jeans. The experiment did not last long. Carter committed the error of announcing that he would immure himself in the White House for the duration of the Iranian hostage crisis. This vow, which he ultimately broke, reinforced the manufactured perception that America, including its chief executive, was being held hostage by the lawless and fanatical Tehran street mob. Probably, the major consequence of this experiment in self-imprisonment, soon abandoned, was that it provided

President Dwight D. Eisenhower stands at the door of the presidential helicopter on the South Lawn of the White House. Helicopters enable presidents and others to enter and leave the White House without dealing with Washington's congested traffic. Courtesy of the National Park Service, from the Dwight D. Eisenhower Library.

a model against which Carter's successor could, and would, react —
with a vengeance.

The Reagan years saw the pursuit of a political agenda frankly keyed
to visual values. Words and sometimes even facts were at a discount. In
one famous case, Lesley Stahl of CBS News did what she regarded as a
scathing evening news piece on the Reagan presidency. She was con-
gratulated on it by the presidential image-makers, who knew that the
true test was how good the president looked in the pictures. The supreme symbol was the East Room press conference, where the president
approached the waiting reporters along a long red carpet, as in an imperial audience. The settings of power and authority overshadowed the
substance on these relatively rare occasions. The president's policy or
agenda might appear, at times, indistinct or muddled. But the symbols
of presidential authority, and the White House itself, were shown to
great advantage.

II

Before 1975 I had known the White House only as an occasional tourist
and from afar. That changed when I came to Washington in June of that
year to be editorial page editor of the *Washington Star*. Gerald Ford was
in the White House, though not for long. It was the White House of his
successor, Jimmy Carter, that I came to know at first hand. Perhaps,
drawing upon those few occasional experiences, I can give a more immediate picture of how the Executive Mansion is used as a political
instrument.

Carter initially distanced himself from the Washington press corps.
He viewed it, with some reason, as an arm of the Washington-insider
culture that he hoped to disregard and even to set on its ear. For practical
reasons, however, he soon changed his mind and decided that he needed
to know more about the Washington press, and we about him. The consequence of this change of heart was a welcome invitation to dine privately, one July night in 1978, in the upstairs family quarters. We made
a party of about ten, the editors of the *Washington Star* and of *Time*
magazine and our wives.

The president was waiting to greet us in the foyer of the south ground-
floor entrance; one by one we all took our turns being photographed

This informal press conference hosted by President Jimmy Carter (right, foreground) on the South Lawn of the White House reflected his style. Such small gatherings, unlike large televised conferences, allow the president to test reactions to possible initiatives. Courtesy of the White House Historical Association.

with him. Then we went upstairs to the sitting area in the west end of the private quarters, just under the great fan-shaped window. It was a bright, sunny evening, and we sat there in the heady radiance of it all, sipping, if I recall, gin and orange juice — though I am not sure the gin was encouraged. The conversation turned to the president's recent meetings with European leaders, to whom he referred, I noticed with mild surprise, by their first names: "Valéry" (Giscard d'Estaing), "Jim" (Callaghan), and "Helmut" (Schmidt). If there was an agenda for the evening, beyond getting better acquainted, the president artfully concealed it. I suppose the subtext was the president's hope for more sympathetic ears. But with Carter there hardly ever seemed to be a sharply pointed message. After dinner Mrs. Carter led the ladies on a tour of the Lincoln bedroom and other notable points of interest in the private quarters. All of us then checked out the view from the Truman balcony, and soon a pleasant evening came to an end. It was, in some sense, a political event, no doubt, but the ultimate purpose was veiled in hospitality.

One Saturday morning a year or so later, the president assembled, again in the upstairs sitting room, a small group of Washington newspeople. The Persian Gulf question was in the news, for the shah of Iran, mainstay of our position in that region, was beginning to totter on the Peacock Throne. A Saturday morning briefing is — fortunately — unusual. But you do not bicker over an invitation to have Saturday-morning breakfast with the president. As we sat there in a circle, the president talked discursively about the Gulf and the Middle East. I seem to have missed the point, at least as one seasoned and imaginative member of our group discerned it. Hedrick Smith, then the *New York Times* Washington correspondent, wrote a front-page backgrounder in the next day's Sunday *Times*. The gist of it was that a "Carter Doctrine" for the Gulf was evolving within administration circles and being tested by the very highest sources, who could not be named. We apparently served as a sounding board for an almost casual presidential enunciation of what he would stress as a vital interest. Of course, the Gulf had been just that since the British, nearly a decade earlier, had abandoned their historic role east of Suez. I am not, to this day, certain how much of this new Carter Doctrine had been clearly formed by that Saturday morning and how much of it was the product of Rick Smith's interpretive genius.

President Carter was thought, by some, to be somewhat casual in some diplomatic matters. Simcha Dinitz, at that period the Israeli ambassador in Washington, once said with some amusement that so far as the Israelis could tell, the first presidential expression of interest in a Palestinian "homeland" or "entity" had come between innings of a softball game in Plains, Georgia.

My notes for this occasion have vanished into a file somewhere. But I am reasonably confident that the Carter Doctrine for the Gulf, enunciated right under my nose, was foggier in the briefing than it later became. Certainly, I left the session that morning blissfully unaware that it had been historic. I did not realize its momentousness until I was telephoned, first thing Monday morning, by the late John Osborne, the superb "White House Watch" reporter for the *New Republic*. Osborne had not been present; but he was on the scent. Was it true, he asked, that I had been among those present to hear the Carter Doctrine declared? I had been, but I had to confess to Osborne that the president's little talk had seemed to me a good deal less sharply focused than Rick Smith's enterprising interpretation made it seem. Still, the coffee and the company were exceptional, and I was glad to have been included. I have an autographed photo.

I now move on to a yet more puzzling example of White House hospitality. One bright Friday morning in early May 1980, some days after the Desert One hostage rescue attempt failed, my phone rang. It was by then 11:00 A.M., and a few minutes later, I would have been on my way downtown to a luncheon reunion of the White House Fellows, where friends had asked me to speak. Now, however, Jody Powell was on the phone. He apologized for the short notice and said "the boss" had a bit of time in an hour and would like me to come to a small lunch. Of course, I made my excuses and went. It turned out to be my most interesting glimpse of President Carter within these legendary precincts. There were only two other guests, Meg Greenfield of the *Washington Post*, and the columnist Carl Rowan. It was a warm, sunny day, and the luncheon table had been set on the terrace just outside the Oval Office. I also have a photograph of this occasion, and I looked at it, for the first time in years, the other day. The three of us seem to be straining forward, just a bit, to catch what the president is saying. Again, the agenda was muted. President Carter was still licking the wounds of the Desert One calamity and trying to come to terms philosophically with the harsh things his critics were saying. He talked about the close emotional bond he had formed with Colonel Beckwith, the leader of the special strike force, who had told him, "Mr. President, you're as tough as a woodpecker's beak." Perhaps that was the message we were expected to carry away from this pleasant, if impromptu, occasion. Carter had lost his secretary of state, Cyrus Vance, who had resigned over the rescue attempt. He had named Senator Edmund Muskie — an appointment, I understood him to say, he had discussed only with Mrs. Carter.

I expect our eyebrows must have risen a bit at that. Within an hour or so, the president excused himself and left. Nothing really reportable had been said — or, if it had been, none of us had been making notes, and none of the usual ground rules had been mentioned. After a brief huddle, the three of us decided that the event had been social and should be treated as such. We made a sort of pact that none of us would write about it then, and none of us did. Still, it was a treat to have lunch at, or just outside, the nation's most famous office. No doubt there was a presidential agenda of some sort involved. This was not the only occasion when that was unclear. One day, Murray Gart, the editor in chief of the *Star*, and I were summoned to the White House by Hamilton Jordan, Carter's chief of staff. There was to be, Ham said, a briefing on some new Middle East initiative. We sat there in Jordan's office while he paced nervously about, occasionally dialing an internal White House number to find out whether Zbigniew Brzezinski, Carter's national security adviser, had completed the briefing he was giving elsewhere so that he could come to us. Jordan kept apologizing that he couldn't tell us much about the matter, but "Zbig" could and would, and he would be there soon. Like Godot, he never came. We waited as long as we could. Then we had to return to the *Star* unbriefed.

With the departure of President Carter in 1981, a brief season of frequent access to the White House ended for me, except for an occasional mass breakfast arranged by Godfrey Sperling of the *Christian Science Monitor*. These were cordial but not intimate occasions. Indeed, it was a bit like breakfasting in the commons of a resort hotel, with scores in attendance. President Reagan's relaxed morning schedule meant that the briefing rarely began before 9:15 or so. We enjoyed a solid hour of orange juice beforehand. The information level was modest, though the president was invariably cheerful and friendly. One memory stands out. Secretary of State Shultz had brokered a "peace" agreement between Israel and the Gemayel government in Lebanon. But the Lebanese, under Syrian pressure, seemed to be retreating from their commitment. My colleague Phil Geyelin, formerly editorial page editor of the *Washington Post* and a seasoned student of Middle East diplomacy, asked President Reagan a question about this now bedraggled pact: What, if anything, was his administration doing to see that the agreement was observed?

"Oh," said the president airily, "we regard it as an agreement between the parties themselves, and making it work is entirely their business." This is a paraphrase; but the sense is, I think, accurate. There was a stir in the room, as there often was when the president seemed to know too little about the vital business of his own administration. At least there was murmuring among those who knew that the secretary of state was deeply involved in the agreement, took intense pride in it, and was keenly determined to see that it amounted to more than a scrap of paper. Many were thinking, I suspect, that they would have to scrape George Shultz off the wall on the State Department's seventh floor when the secretary of state learned of this hands-off presidential position. I was not surprised to hear on the car radio, an hour or so later, that the White House had "clarified" the president's remark, making it very clear that the United States was actively interested in the observance of the agreement.

III

One might gather from these too-sketchy reminiscences that when seen at ground level, the uses of the White House to advance presidential agendas can be less clear than they sometimes seem to be from outside it. My experience was obviously very limited; but I suspect that others would say the same. The daily reality of the White House is often somewhat truer to these modest experiences, in which presidential agendas are not clearly defined, than it is to the efficient, purposeful, powerhouse impression that is produced — in the theatrical sense — by those who surround presidents today with lights, music, and greasepaint.

It is not often, I think, a matter so much of deliberate deception as of the almost universal tendency, in the television age, for operational realities at every level of government to depart from the impressions we have of them. They are necessarily complex and full of verbal shadings and qualifications. The mediated visual impression is done, necessarily, in broad strokes and bright primary colors.

The White House may be seen not only as a historic house, in which, with imagination, one still catches the echoes of the playing Roosevelt children, but also as the workplace and residence of a busy and, of course, limited and less than superhuman chief executive. The theater is always there; what were novelties in President Eisenhower's day are regarded as necessities today. There is a programmatic presidency and a long agenda to go with it; they bear all the earmarks of the TV age, with all the self-importance, self-promotion, and pomp they seem to have. "The White House says . . ." are still perhaps the weightiest words in Washington. But in my own limited view, the real presidency behind this facade is, sometimes surprisingly, groping for definition. One is reminded of a scene from a famous American movie, when an irreverent little dog pulls aside the curtain in the Emerald City, and the wonderful Wizard of Oz turns out to be an ordinary man from Kansas. No insult to the dignity of a great house and a great office is intended, but that's the way the White House sometimes seemed to me as well.

NOTES

George Reedy's essay in this volume includes a useful list of works on the presidency and the press. In addition, interested readers should see Edwin M. Yoder, Jr., *The Unmaking of a Whig and Other Essays in Self-Definition* (Washington: Georgetown University Press, 1990).

1. Constance McLaughlin Green, *Washington: A History of the Capital, 1800–1950* (Princeton, N.J.: Princeton University Press, 1976).

2. See Edward S. Corwin, *The President: Office and Powers 1787–1957*, 4th ed. (New York: New York University Press, 1957), 264: "The nationalization of American industry, the necessity of curbing monopolistic practices . . . the conservation movement of the first Roosevelt, the rise and consolidation of the labor movement, the altered outlook on the proper scope of governmental func-

tions that the Great Depression produced, and finally two great wars and their aftermath have all conspired to thrust into the foreground of our constitutional system the dual role of the President as catalyst of public opinion and as legislative leader." It is the latter presidential function that might be called "programmatic" in the sense intended.

3. George F. Will, *Restoration* (New York: The Free Press, 1992), 131.

4. See "Johnson and the Election Campaign of 1866," chap. 13 in Eric L. McKitrick, *Andrew Johnson and Reconstruction* (Chicago: University of Chicago Press, 1964), 421 ff.

5. The "front-porch" campaign of William McKinley in 1896 is generally regarded as the classic instance. See Margaret Leech, *In the Days of McKinley* (New York: Harper & Brothers, 1959), 87–88: "McKinley's conception of his candidacy was so passive that he gave the impression of intending to make no campaign at all. . . . Except for three days' absence to keep . . . appointments and one week of rest in August, McKinley remained in Canton [his hometown in Ohio] from the date of his nomination until the election. . . . He may have been influenced by the example set by Benjamin Harrison in 1892, but the idea of the 'front-porch campaign' seems to have been a natural outgrowth of the many groups that visited Canton."

6. Joseph W. Alsop, *I've Seen the Best of It* (New York: W. W. Norton & Co., 1992), 136.

7. Ibid., 137.

8. Fred I. Greenstein, *The Hidden-Hand Presidency* (New York: Basic Books, 1982), 96, 146.

9. Charles Roberts, "Kennedy and the Press: Image and Reality," in *The Kennedy Presidency*, ed. Kenneth W. Thompson (Lanham, Md., and London: University Press of America, 1985), chap. 5.

Chapter

10

The First Lady's
Changing Role

Betty Boyd Caroli

No topic in American politics offers a more interesting contradiction than the role of the presidential spouse. This is not a job in the sense that it is paid, yet it is full-time work. It results from a private relationship yet becomes the subject of considerable public attention. Political scientists frequently ignore it, but individual First Ladies — even candidates for the job — become the focus of innumerable magazine articles, television interviews, and books that quickly climb to the top of the best-seller list. The same newspapers that choose not to review books on the subject of First Ladies, even those from the oldest, most scholarly presses, will run front-page articles on an individual First Lady whenever she makes a speech, takes a trip, or catches the flu. It is not surprising that historian Lewis Gould concluded: "The First Lady is an institution in American government that is as important as it is ill-defined."[1]

Not content to incorporate a First Lady into their own political system, Americans have exported the title to very different kinds of governments without translating it out of English. If Italians made "prima donna" an international phrase, Americans can take credit for inventing "First Lady." In foreign newspapers we have learned to read, without raising an eyebrow, of First Ladies in political systems as diverse as those of the Philippines under Marcos, Haiti during the Duvalier regime, and the Soviet Union of Raisa and Mikhail Gorbachev. The Americans who held the title may have detested it, and Jacqueline Kennedy initially forbade use of the term, which she found more appropriate to a saddle horse. But it has persisted all the same.

In spite of their claim to the invention, Americans have been reluctant to study the role of the First Lady, and the recent scholarly attention results from several concurrent developments. The presidential libraries, with their newly opened files on additional parts of White House operations, have provided the materials with which to analyze the many facets of an administration. White House social files, long ignored as legitimate subjects of study, are being looked at anew to see what they will yield about a president's approach to the job. The First Lady's appointment books, speaking schedules, and guest lists add to the record of any administration. Does it not add to our understanding of the presidency of Herbert Hoover to read the letter that his wife, known for her appreciation of fine horses, wrote thanking a man who had just volunteered to give the Hoovers a new Cadillac? First Lady Lou Hoover wrote: "We make a strict rule . . . of not accepting the many 'commercial' presents that are so kindly offered us. But in some way we feel differently about this prancing new little steed. She seems so much like a new colt just come prancing in from the pasture. . . . And there seems so much of personality woven into its makeup, that I cannot resist adding it to my Cadillac stable."[2]

Changes in women's history, moving it beyond its relatively narrow focus of the 1960s and 1970s, have also nurtured the new interest in presidential spouses. So long as women's history concentrated only on women as primary actors — in movements aimed at achieving suffrage, implementing reforms, and improving working conditions — it was not likely to look at the more subtle kinds of ways women were involved in politics, including their influence in the White House. These last few years have witnessed a redefinition of women's political activity, expanding it beyond simply voting and holding office so that it considers other ways that women carved out public roles and affected life outside their homes.

This new approach enables us to view a nineteenth-century First Lady, such as Sarah Polk, in a different light and to perceive similarities between her and Hillary Clinton that might have otherwise escaped us. Like Mrs. Clinton, Mrs. Polk evidently preferred discussions of public policy to those of domesticity and was not shy about saying so. To those who objected in 1992 to Hillary Clinton's statement about giving low priority to cookie baking, it is instructive to note that Sarah Polk was challenged in the 1844 election by a man who said he would vote for her husband's opponent, Henry Clay, because Mrs. Clay made better butter than Mrs. Polk. The latter countered that if she got to the White House, she would live on $25,000 a year (the salary of the chief executive at the time) and would neither make butter nor keep house.[3] James Polk's biographers concluded that she kept her word and acted during her husband's presidency as an adviser and confidante.

In addition to these two changes at the presidential libraries and in the study of women's history, the last few decades have shown new rules for winning elections and conducting a successful presidency. Americans have come to accept the fact that the candidate's wife and children will be packaged as part of the campaign, and a president's family, especially those members who reside in the White House, will be scrutinized, tutored, and implicated in any evaluation of an administration. The presidency now seems to extend to an entire family. How else can we explain the public attention given to Amy Carter's school choice, Nancy Reagan's wardrobe, and Chelsea Clinton's cat?

The latest writing on First Ladies describes a large public role. Journal articles, doctoral dissertations, and heavily footnoted volumes generally agree that the first two centuries of the nation's history have seen a progression from a largely ceremonial figure to a position of potentially great power.[4] Disagreement exists only on the timing of the change and the degree to which the role has become institutionalized rather than being dependent on the personalities and the interests of those who hold the job. Authors generally concur on four components of the First Lady's job: campaigner; communicator for the chief executive; complement to, or extension of, the president's program; and curator of the President's House.

Perhaps the most striking change in the job is in the race to get it — the extent to which candidates' wives campaign too. This is a recent development. Until the 1960s, speaking out for one's husband in any kind of partisan way was considered inappropriate. In 1928 Lou Hoover wrote to thank a donor for sending campaign buttons promoting Herbert

Hoover's candidacy, but she explained that neither she nor any member of her family would wear one.[5] Even the path-breaking Eleanor Roosevelt hesitated to make a partisan statement in favor of her husband.[6] Bess Truman did little more than nod in acknowledgment when her husband introduced her as "The Boss" to crowds gathered to greet his campaign train. In 1952 Mamie Eisenhower lent her name as author to an article in *Good Housekeeping* asking readers to "Vote for My Husband or for Governor Stevenson but Please Vote."[7]

Then this kind of reticent nonpartisanship vanished. In the 1960 presidential campaign, both major parties involved the candidates' wives. After Jacqueline Kennedy went out on a few short trips, the Women's Division of the Republican National Committee set up special events featuring Pat Nixon. Press releases emphasized Mrs. Nixon's value to the ticket, and the Republicans scheduled a "Pat week" of coffees and mini-rallies where she appeared.[8] In 1964 Lady Bird Johnson journeyed on her own through the southern states on a train dubbed the Lady Bird Special. She was accompanied by her daughters, her advisers, and her indomitable chief of staff, Liz Carpenter, but her husband remained back in Washington.[9]

In the 1970s Rosalynn Carter advanced the idea of wife as campaigner when she went out on her own and worked full-time for Jimmy Carter's nomination more than a year before the convention.[10] By the 1980s spouses were expected to involve themselves early and fully in the campaign — even if they had full-time careers of their own. In July 1987 — twelve months before the Democrats nominated their standard-bearer — the wives of six hopefuls met on a stage in Des Moines, Iowa, in a large room packed with television cameras and print journalists from across the nation and even abroad, each to speak about how her husband would make the best candidate.

This remarkable meeting occurred exactly two hundred years after the Constitutional Convention debated the novel invention of the presidency, and it is safe to say that none of the Founding Fathers could have predicted such a gathering as that in Des Moines. But, then, the delegates to the Constitutional Convention would have been equally surprised by the role of candidates' wives at the 1992 Republican convention where, for the first time, the spouses of both nominees addressed the delegates.

To understand the importance of spouses enthusiastically participating in the campaign, it is perhaps useful to ask what would happen if they did not. How would voters greet the news that the husband or wife of a presidential candidate refused to give interviews, make speeches, take part in photo opportunities, or release family pictures? It is difficult to imagine that taking such a position in 1992 would not have a negative impact on the candidacy.

Once the campaign is over and the victory secure, the winner's spouse immediately faces a job of several dimensions — one for which there is no exact job description but plenty of critics and lots of press attention. She has considerable latitude to stress those parts of the job with which she feels most comfortable or has the greatest expertise and preparation. None has followed Eleanor Roosevelt's practice of holding weekly news conferences for women reporters, although several have had occasional meetings with the press when some particular topic needed clarification or exposure. None has imitated Rosalynn Carter by traveling abroad as the president's emissary to discuss substantive matters, such as trade policy and defense, although several have made ceremonial visits. Whether she will attend cabinet meetings, make public her own disagreements with the chief executive's policies, reveal her own assessments of the president's staff and scheduling — these are decisions that every administration, or some part of it, makes for itself.

But no incumbent can deny the communicator aspect of being First Lady — a function that has become particularly visible in the twentieth century. One doctoral dissertation, subsequently published as a book with a slightly different title, focused on the partnership in the presidency, especially as "Public Communicator."[11] Author Myra Gutin argued that enormous changes between 1920 and 1970, including developments in radio and television as well as in women's roles and the public's expectations, helped move the job of First Lady beyond that of being simply a "White Housekeeper" who was "Social Hostess and Ceremonial Presence." By 1961 that model had been superseded by the "Incipient Spokeswoman" who presented herself as a "Visible Helpmate," or even as a "Political Surrogate and Independent Advocate." Gutin is

President and Mrs. Carter receive Pope John Paul II. Courtesy of the White House Historical Association.

meticulous in citing the number of speeches given, miles traveled, and persons reached by First Ladies in their public communicator roles.

The women themselves have underlined this part of the role. Since 1963 all but one of the First Ladies have published their autobiographies, and the one who did not — Pat Nixon — had the job performed admirably for her by her daughter. Every one stressed the role of communicator in one of its many different forms. Lady Bird Johnson and Rosalynn Carter wrote of working to overcome their fear of public speaking; Julie Nixon Eisenhower enumerated her mother's solo trips to Venezuela, Brazil, Liberia, and Ghana.[12] Nancy Reagan emphasized the size of the "platform" given presidential spouses,[13] and Betty Ford explained how she came to understand the opportunity to reach people on subjects as diverse as going for medical examinations and raising teenage daughters. "Lying in the hospital," Betty Ford wrote after her mastectomy in 1974, "thinking of all those women going for cancer checkups because of me, I'd come to recognize more clearly the power of the woman in the White House. Not my power, but the power of the position, a power which could be used to help."[14]

The extent of communication has increased in our century, but the foundation for it was there from the beginning. No nineteenth-century incumbent could have come close to the record of a Pat Nixon or Eleanor Roosevelt in the number of miles flown or people seen and touched. Yet First Ladies of the 1800s had their own ways of reaching out. Before the Civil War, they were largely local figures, rarely seen outside Washington, but then national magazines helped make them recognizable to most Americans. Lucy Hayes found a warm welcome when she became the first to travel across the continent, and Frances Cleveland's photo appeared in advertisements for a variety of products.

The communicator role clearly precedes modern transportation and national magazines, and it has its roots in the letters of appeal that reached presidents' wives from the earliest days of the Republic. Presidential libraries are full of such letters, and biographies of nineteenth-century men and women report them. The Native Americans and artists who approached Harriet Lane (bachelor James Buchanan's niece and First Lady) and the Mormons and temperance workers who appealed to Lucy Hayes underline the very old role of First Lady as communicator.

Beyond the communicating role, the First Lady has the opportunity to serve as an extension of the president — to expand his agenda and complement his program. Most Americans presumably know better than the immigrant interviewed in the 1920s about his understanding of his new country's government. When asked who would succeed President Harding, the immigrant replied: "the president's wife." Newcomers in the 1990s are undoubtedly more familiar with the job of vice president, but they also know a great deal about the president's wife. After all, a major newspaper recently concluded that Nancy Reagan had elevated the job of First Lady to that of an associate presidency.[15]

Sometimes this associate presidency role means filling in or balancing. If the chief executive is perceived as preoccupied with foreign policy or uncaring about education, a spouse can compensate by making speeches and organizing conferences. When he is sick, she can appear in his place. She has the chance to give opinions, influence appointments, and affect scheduling. In the 1930s, Molly Dewson, head of the Women's Division of the Democratic National Committee, told of her debt to Eleanor Roosevelt. Whenever she needed to discuss something with the president, Dewson spoke to the First Lady, who arranged for the two to sit next to each other at dinner. "The matter was settled," Dewson wrote, "before we finished our soup."[16]

Since 1961 every First Lady has selected a project or special cause as her own — and the association between the woman and the project became so well known that decades after that First Lady leaves Washington, her name is linked in Americans' minds with a particular subject: Jacqueline Kennedy and White House restoration; Lady Bird Johnson and beautification; Pat Nixon and volunteerism; Betty Ford and the Equal Rights Amendment (and also modern dance); Rosalynn Carter and mental health; Nancy Reagan and anti-drug programs; Barbara Bush and literacy.

This is no frivolous association — the benefits can be enormous. Lewis Gould documented the value of Lady Bird Johnson's beautification program, designed to improve the environment and raise community consciousness on that subject.[17] Nancy Reagan's switch from a Foster Grandparents program to Just Say No to Drugs was accompanied by a twenty-point surge in her popularity.[18] At least part of Barbara Bush's high rating in the polls could be attributed to the public perception that she really cared about whether or not the nation's children could read.

The large staffs necessary for a successful program are relatively new. Not until 1961 did a First Lady have her own press secretary, but then the staff numbers spiraled — although it is difficult to quantify the exact size of the East Wing office, since so many of the staff come on loan from other departments or agencies, remaining on that other payroll until the job is finished. Yet each First Lady since 1963 has employed a sizable retinue of persons who deal with the press, promote the association of the First Lady with a cause or mission by scheduling speeches and trips, and look for ways to maximize her contribution to the administration. Rumors of frictions between the East and West Wings, buttressed by examples of how very bitter the conflict can become, underline the fact that the First Lady's office is a separate, albeit complementary, part of the presidency.

In looking for the origins of this associate presidency role, some students of the subject have emphasized the competence of the women who held the job in the first two centuries — a remarkably able group of women, often coming from social and economic backgrounds considerably superior to their husbands'. Others have dwelt on the institution of the presidency itself, which left open to each incumbent the opportunity to choose advisers at will, without the tight constraints imposed by political parties in a parliamentary system. These observers note that presidents as far back as the second president relied on their wives' counsel, although, in some people's opinion, John Adams did not rely enough on Abigail. His critics charged that he had exercised poor judgment in making one appointment and that if Abigail had been present, the mistake would not have occurred.

Still other students of the First Lady's role have noted the double duty of presidents who act as head of government but also as head of state. Is it any wonder that some presidents have enlisted the help of spouses in the ceremonial tasks? Betty Ford admitted that the largest part of her schedule went to these ceremonial jobs — greeting visitors, getting pictures taken, and standing in for the president.

The fourth public role of every First Lady is that of curator of the nation's most visited home and one of its most photographed museums.

Lady Bird Johnson carries out the First Lady's role as a leader in national movements by conferring with members of her Highway Beautification Committee in the White House Treaty Room. Eleanor Roosevelt's efforts on behalf of underprivileged Americans and Barbara Bush's literacy campaign mark two other instances of First Lady as activist. Courtesy of the White House Historical Association.

Although she has a full-time professional staff to assist her in this role (as she does in the other three mentioned above), it is her taste and her emphasis that Americans associate with the choices made.

If we have some trouble tracing the development of the other parts of her job, that of curator is fairly clear. President Washington's decision to make his residence double as his office helped bring his spouse into the government process. To any two people who both work at home, it is hardly necessary to prove how business overlaps with pleasure — and official visits often overlap with social calls. Many White House occupants have objected to the arrangement. President Arthur insisted that no businessman would consent to live in the same building where he worked,[19] and Edith Roosevelt likened her situation to a storekeeper "living over the store."[20] But none of the White House families ever successfully bucked what quickly became accepted tradition.

The very first occupants of the President's House helped solidify the First Lady's responsibility for the mansion's furnishings. Almost as soon as she had moved in, Abigail Adams lodged her now famous complaints against the building's appearance and lack of comforts. Much remained unfinished, and the few furnishings were bizarre — such as the mirrors that she described as "fit only for dwarfs." Within weeks her husband lost his bid for reelection, and she had to prepare to move out. Widower Thomas Jefferson took little interest in furnishing his temporary quarters, but Dolley Madison, working with the Surveyor of Public Buildings, embarked on a buying spree in order to get the house ready for public receptions. Few Americans got a chance to see what she had done before the British burned the President's House in August 1814. It is safe to say, however, that Dolley Madison helped establish in the public mind the idea that the president's wife had a responsibility for the upkeep of the President's House and for granting people access. Every subsequent First Lady would find her purchases scrutinized for indications of her taste and style and her bills examined for evidence of extravagance or frugality.

No holds are barred, it seems, when royalty spends, but Americans' judgment of a First Lady's buying swings with the times. What is perfectly acceptable at one time is termed crass, insensitive, and vulgar a few years later. Is there any doubt that Jacqueline Kennedy's refurbish-

Former First Lady Barbara Bush presents an award to Safety Patrol members. In the twentieth century, the First Lady's duties and influence have moved beyond such ceremonial functions, but they still constitute an important part of her role. Courtesy of the White House Historical Association.

ing of the Executive Mansion in the early 1960s was regarded far more favorably than Nancy Reagan's decision to purchase new china and upgrade the family quarters twenty years later? Julia Grant's lavish outlays stand in sharp contrast to Lucy Hayes's frugality — a frugality that sent her ferreting in attics to find furniture suitable for use in the White House. Abraham Lincoln tried unsuccessfully to limit his wife's spending, pointing out that it would "stink in the nostrils" of the American people if he were to approve an overrun on White House purchases at a time when Union soldiers went without blankets and adequate clothing.[21]

Presidents' wives have also taken responsibility for initiating studies of the White House and cataloguing its contents. Until the 1960s, when decisions regarding the residence became institutionalized in the White House Historical Association, the Committee for the Preservation of the White House, and the professional curatorial staff, it was the First Ladies, assisted by volunteers and friends, who undertook this work. They were not always successful. Lucretia Garfield's proposed research on the White House and its furnishings was cut short, first by her own illness and then by her husband's assassination. Grace Coolidge named an advisory committee to help her, but then disagreements limited the committee's effectiveness. Scholarly Lou Hoover would have had the mansion's contents catalogued for publication had funding been available.

Since 1961 the public's association of First Ladies with the White House and its contents has become even more firmly entrenched. Jacqueline Kennedy's restoration project, Lady Bird Johnson's appeal to donors of important paintings, Pat Nixon's work to bring back original American pieces rather than reproductions, and Nancy Reagan's upgrading of the living quarters — all got important press coverage.

If the curatorial function is enlarged beyond the building itself to include programming American talent, then the list grows. For nearly a century, First Ladies took responsibility for overseeing musical performances for invited guests. Then Rosalynn Carter explained the decision to carry White House concerts on national television, saying that she knew there were many Americans who would like to come to the White House if they had the chance.

If the writers of the Constitution had been able to foresee the large public role that the presidential spouse would assume, would they have written it in? Not likely. But the document they devised allowed the latitude for it to develop. Since that May day in 1789 when Martha Washington arrived in the temporary capital in New York, the First Lady has had a public role. The Washingtons could have made other arrangements, but the president decided his wife should cross the Hudson River in the presidential barge and then be greeted with a thirteen-gun salute. The public welcome extended to Martha Washington as she moved up Broadway to the rented house that her husband had taken on Cherry Street would be equivalent to a ticker-tape parade two centuries later.

Americans, most of whom knew royalty and their ways only from a considerable distance, could be expected to look for some of the glamour of queens in the woman married to their president, and they trained a critical eye on her clothing, the desserts she served, and the entertainments she favored. Is there any wonder that Lady Washington complained of all the attention and admitted, at the end of her husband's two terms, that she and he felt like "two children let out of school"?

From the distance of two hundred years, it is instructive to look back at the debate that took place soon after Martha Washington arrived to take the job. With no precedent to guide them, New Yorkers remained unsure of her title or of how she should be addressed. Some suggested "Marquise," while others preferred "Lady." Finally, one irate upstater, who chose to use a pen name rather than reveal his identity, wrote to an Albany newspaper to complain. If the current trend continued to focus so much public attention on the president's wife, he argued, sooner or later Americans would be reading something like the following: "Her Serenity who was much indisposed last week by a pain in the third joint of the fourth finger of her left hand . . . is in a fair way of recovery . . . [and went out] in the Siberian fur lately delivered to her by the Russian Ambassador as a present from the Princess."[22] What he predicted in sarcasm in 1789 we have seen occur, as we have come to read newspaper articles about the surgery Nancy Reagan underwent for a small growth on the left side of her nose after going to the hospital in a suit designed by Adolfo.

While the first two centuries of White House history have included a large public role for the First Lady, the third century is sure to hold many changes. Some observers predict that the job as we have known it will disappear as presidential spouses are more likely to be men or women with professional careers that they cannot — or choose not to — put on hold for four years. More probably, the agenda for First Ladies will be enlarged and redefined.

Indeed, Hillary Rodham Clinton indicates how a younger generation of women (born after World War II) sees new potential in the job of presidential spouse. With a set of credentials that rivaled her husband's, she campaigned vigorously for his election. Then, with the inauguration behind her, she took an office in the West Wing, agreed to head the president's task force on improving the nation's health care, and went off to lobby leaders of both parties of Congress. Lest she should be criticized for neglecting her curatorial function and devoting too much time to communicating for her husband and complementing his agenda, she also took time to get herself photographed for the nation's biggest newspapers while inspecting the table arrangements for the Clintons' first formal dinner party. Once again the public role of a First Lady was being reshaped — but on roots that reached back to the beginning of the Republic.

NOTES

1. Lewis Gould, Introduction to *Modern First Ladies: Their Documentary Legacy*, ed. Nancy Kegan Smith and Mary C. Ryan (Washington: National Archives and Records Administration, 1989), 3.

2. Lou Hoover to Lawrence Fisher, May 5, 1929, "Cadillac," Lou Henry Hoover Papers, Hoover Library.

3. Anson Nelson and Fanny Nelson, *Memorials of Sarah Childress Polk* (New York, 1892), 79.

4. Carl Sferrazza Anthony, *First Ladies*, 2 vols. (New York: William Morrow, 1990–1991); Paul F. Boller, *Presidential Wives* (New York: Oxford University Press, 1988); Betty Boyd Caroli, *First Ladies* (New York: Oxford University Press, 1987); Myra Gutin, *The President's Partner: The First Lady in the Twentieth Century* (Westport, Conn.: Greenwood Press, 1989); Smith and Ryan, eds., *Modern First Ladies*. In addition to these book-length studies of the subject, see *Presidential Studies Quarterly*, which devoted half of its Fall 1990 issue to the theme "Modern First Ladies."

5. Lou Hoover to Mr. Muller, July 25, 1928, "1928 Campaign," Lou Henry Hoover Papers, Hoover Library.

6. Joseph P. Lash, *Love, Eleanor: Eleanor Roosevelt and Her Friends* (Garden City, N.Y.: Doubleday, 1982), 131.

7. Mamie Eisenhower, "Vote for My Husband or for Governor Stevenson but Please Vote," *Good Housekeeping* (November 1952), 13.

8. Julie Nixon Eisenhower, *Pat Nixon: The Untold Story* (New York: Simon & Schuster, 1986), 189–90.

9. Lady Bird Johnson, *A White House Diary* (New York: Holt, Rinehart and Winston, 1970), 195–98.

10. Rosalynn Carter, *First Lady from Plains* (Boston: Houghton Mifflin Co., 1984), 112–35.

11. Myra Gutin, *The President's Partner: The First Lady in the Twentieth Century,* first appeared as "The President's Partner: The First Lady as Public Communicator, 1920–1976" (Ph.D. diss., University of Michigan, 1983).

12. Julie Eisenhower, *Pat Nixon,* 329–30, 403–4.

13. Nancy Reagan (with William Novak), *My Turn: The Memoirs of Nancy Reagan* (New York: Random House, 1989), 57.

14. Betty Ford (with Chris Chase), *The Times of My Life* (New York: Harper & Row, 1978), 194.

15. *New York Times,* July 13, 1986, E7.

16. Susan Ware, *Holding Their Own: American Women in the 1930s* (Boston: G. K. Hall & Co., 1982), 91.

17. Lewis Gould, *Lady Bird Johnson and the Environment* (Lawrence: University Press of Kansas, 1988).

18. *New York Times,* March 26, 1985, A20.

19. John Tebbel and Sarah Miles Watt, *The Press and the Presidency: From George Washington to Ronald Reagan* (New York: Oxford University Press, 1985), 251.

20. Sylvia Jukes Morris, *Edith Kermit Roosevelt: Portrait of a First Lady* (New York: Coward, McCann & Geoghegan, 1980), 222.

21. William Seale, *The President's House,* 2 vols. (Washington: White House Historical Association, 1986), 1:390.

22. *Daily Advertiser,* June 15, 1789, 1.

11

Music at the White House:

Legacy of American Romanticism

Elise K. Kirk

The White House is the nation's oldest showcase for the performing arts — and a stage like no other in the world.[1] As both home and office of the president of the United States, it is private, domestic, and intimate, but at the same time public, visible, and powerfully linked with the people.

Few edifices in the world can boast the variety and excellence of its music, yet few theaters have been so conditioned by changing political attitudes. No other aspect of White House life can define the presidential image quite like the music performed at the chief of state's residence. Powerful, elusive, joyous, persuasive, poignant, elegant, and brash, White House musical life is a true mirror of America, a glimpse of court life in a democracy — a barometer of our own irrational, secular, romantic spirit.

There is a part of each of us in the music that is performed at the White House: our joy in intimate music making, our pride in ceremony and pageantry, and our thrill in hearing the world's finest performing artists in concert. Where else but at the White House can one find this trio of functions, this *Gebrauchsmusik*, or "useful" music, embodied in a single institution? And if we search a bit deeper into these traditions, we find they are just as vital today as they were in the earliest days of the White House — but with a wonderfully rich and rare distinction.

They have become more and more attuned to the American spirit. Through the long skein of White House musical traditions, we follow our nation as it gradually came to accept and cherish its indigenous creative treasures and depend less and less on European culture. Thus, through the musical history of the White House and its bonds with American romanticism, we witness the gradual shaping of the American national character.

Precisely what *is* American romanticism? Indeed, few scholars and literary historians have concerned themselves with the concept, or even acknowledged its existence. Romanticism, as commonly perceived, was an artistic and philosophical movement that originated in Europe in the late eighteenth century and stretched forward to influence several generations through its Dionysian cult of nature, innermost emotional expression, and personal freedom. More than any other society, the United States has felt the powerful impact of romanticism. But it has also surpassed it. For the myths and symbols of American romanticism are those of a self-proclaimed democracy, whose mission is a never-ending quest for its own identity. As Daniel Boorstin notes: "America . . . flourished not in discovery, but in search. . . . It lived with the constant belief that something else or something better might turn up. . . . When before had men put so much faith in the unexpected?"[2]

American romanticism, David Morse claims, is born of "excessive hopes," manifested especially in the arts, which are "imperiously summoned into existence, like a genie out of a bottle, and expected to expand sensationally before the spectator's very eyes."[3] "Free of feudal shackles and restrictions," writes Morse, America and its arts "would soar as dramatically into the empyrean as the bald-headed eagle itself." While Morse is concerned mainly with literature, his words apply to music as well. America would not only be different from Europe, it would surpass and excel Europe in every way. But, continues Morse, "In ᴏke game with Europe the Americans needed every ounce of bluff ᴛ they could muster."[4] Thus, to American theaters —
ᴜse — would come the unconstrained ballad sing-
ᴛars, the ingenious humbug of P. T. Barnum,
Philip Sousa, and the budding brassy

But let us turn now to the White House itself, for we will note that a kaleidoscope of musical traditions was apparent from the earliest days of the presidency. George Washington not only enjoyed numerous musical plays in New York and Philadelphia, but gave his talented step-granddaughter, Nelly Custis, a fine piano — one of the first items purchased for the president's home and one of the first pianos built in America.⁵ Music was so important to the life and spirit of the early White House that only a few weeks after John and Abigail Adams took residency in the new mansion, the United States Marine Band performed for their first reception on New Year's Day, 1801.⁶ Later that year, for Jefferson's July Fourth celebration, the U.S. Marine Band accompanied the fine singing of Captain Thomas Tingey, first commandant of the Navy Yard — and the earliest known soloist to perform at the White House. And so from the time of Jefferson to the present day the U.S. Marine Band has been called "The President's Own" and has performed regularly at the White House.

Thomas Jefferson was a great devotee of the arts. He was a talented violinist whose extensive collection of music, housed at the University of Virginia, includes the works of Corelli, Haydn, Vivaldi, and Handel. Jefferson once claimed that music was "the favorite passion of my soul" and furnished "a delightful recreation for the hours of respite from the cares of the day."⁷ Dolley Madison occasionally served as Jefferson's hostess, and when she became First Lady in 1809, the White House saw some of the most brilliant social life of its early history. Music played such an important role in Mrs. Madison's household that she purchased for the White House not only a piano, but an elegantly engraved collection of music published by Madame Le Pelletier.⁸ Who was this mysterious lady? We may never know, but her own fine compositions that grace the collection mark her as one of America's earliest women composers.

Dolley Madison also enjoyed dancing and is considered the first to have introduced social dancing to the White House — notably the waltz, called somewhat derisively at this time "the hugging process set to music." Another early president who enjoyed dancing was Martin Van Buren, who, like Jefferson, was a widower. But Van Buren's interest in theatrical, rather than social, dance — especially the performa

the great prima ballerina, Fanny Elssler. With her voluptuous, hip-sway-
ing *cachucha*, complete with Spanish castanets, Elssler was taking all
of Washington by storm at the time. So popular was the provocative
Fanny, in fact, that Congress decided to meet only on the days when she
was *not* dancing. After one of Elssler's performances, President Van
Buren invited the pretty dancer to the White House. "I think his de-
meanor is very easy, very frank and very royal," noted Elssler respect-
fully.⁹ Not all agreed, and the president's "royal" attitude became the
subject of satire and song as the 1840 campaign progressed.

For sheer joy and relaxation, many of our early presidents played musical instruments. John Quincy Adams played the flute; and Jefferson
and John Tyler, and later Woodrow Wilson, played the violin. Tyler even
had a family orchestra, which, with his fifteen children, would not have
been too difficult. Almost half of our nineteenth-century First Ladies
played the piano, notably John Quincy Adams's wife, Louisa Catherine
Adams, who derived great comfort from playing and singing. Before the
days of radio, television, and other forms of mass communication, people often had to make music themselves if they wanted to hear it at all.

The long tradition of inviting guest artists to perform in the White
House — common even today — began during the administration of
John Tyler. The composer John Hill Hewitt tells this funny story about
the legendary pianist Anthony Philip Heinrich, who came to play for
President Tyler. Heinrich, known as "America's Beethoven," wrote
such complex music that few in those days could play it. Right in the
middle of his long, intense piano performance, the president yawned,
rose, and interrupted the frenzied pianist with the request, "Pardon me,
sir, but couldn't you just play a good Virginia reel?" Heinrich did not
know any, and, shocked, left the White House, turned to his friend, and
said: "Mein Gott in Himmel! The people who made John Tyler President ought to be hung! He knows no more about music than an oyster!"¹⁰ John Tyler *did* know a good bit about music — certainly more
than Ulysses S. Grant, who once admitted: "I know only two tunes —
one is Yankee Doodle and the other isn't."¹¹

Few presidents in history have been as deeply moved by music as
Abraham Lincoln. Lincoln was actually a very unmusical president in
the sense that he did not play an instrument, sing, or read music. But

his love of music was a passion. The Hutchinson Family Singers sang their songs of patriotism, abolition, and social injustice for Lincoln. This type of ballad, friends said, brought mist to the president's eyes and "threw him into a fit of deep melancholy."[12] But Lincoln's special love was grand opera. He saw at least thirty fully staged productions while he was president. When he was criticized for attending the opera so much during the turbulent years of the Civil War, he said simply: "I must have a change of some sort or I will die" — a poignant tribute to music's enduring therapeutic powers.[13] Abraham Lincoln was also the first to invite an opera singer to entertain in the White House: the young Meda Blanchard from Washington, D.C., who sang informally in the Red Room in 1861. These were indeed romantic years in America — years when opera and concert stars were advertised as the musical wonders of the world. But did it really matter whether the great De Begnis could sing three hundred bars of music in a minute, as he claimed? The thrill lay in the anticipating, the daring — the emboldening promise that Americans took for granted as their undisputed right.

When master conjurer Phineas T. Barnum brought Jenny Lind, the Swedish Nightingale, to America in 1850, she rapidly became the nation's first superstar. President Millard Fillmore and his family were so thrilled when they heard her at the National Theater that they immediately invited her to visit them in the White House. Years later Barnum himself came to the White House, bringing another singer, the celebrated midget known as "Commodore Nutt," who sang "Columbia the Gem of the Ocean" for Abraham Lincoln and his family in the Red Room.[14]

The most amazing musical program of the post–Civil War era was that of the young black coloratura soprano Marie Selika, who entertained President and Mrs. Rutherford Hayes. Called the "Queen of Staccato," Selika had a fascinating career because America during the frenetic years of Reconstruction was barely ready to accept the black performer outside the rather degrading confines of the minstrel show. So she had gone to Europe to pursue her career and had even sung before crowned heads of state.[15] When she sang for the Hayeses on November 18, 1878, she inaugurated a beautiful tradition at the White House — the "musicale," a short concert with social overtones that was popular

Coloratura soprano Marie Selika appears to have been the first black artist to perform at the White House. She is depicted here in an 1877 engraving by Frederick Carnes. Courtesy of the Music Division, Library of Congress.

in Europe at the time. While the term is no longer used at the White House, the concept remains a graceful vestige of romanticism and vital part of modern White House life.

Not all presidents had such lofty artistic tastes as Rutherford Hayes, however. Grover Cleveland was the only president in history to have served two nonconsecutive terms in office (1885–1889 and 1893–1897) and the only president to be married in the White House. On June 23, 1886, he married the beautiful and charming Frances Folsom, and because she was twenty-one and he was forty-nine, the tongues did wag! Grand opera was really *not* Grover Cleveland's cup of tea, but he did like the new Gilbert and Sullivan operettas that were all the rage in America. He even asked the leader of the U.S. Marine Band, John Philip Sousa, to play parts of the *Mikado* at his White House wedding reception. What did they play? Of course — the ever-popular "Oh, He's Going to Marry Yum-Yum."[16]

As the century turned, new voices were in the air. Times were changing. Presidential power was reactivating. When President Theodore Roosevelt and his wife, Edith, took residency in the White House in 1901, they recognized the important role that music played in the life of the nation — whether Scott Joplin's daring new "Maple Leaf Rag," played by the U.S. Marine Band, or the Boccherini sonata performed by the twenty-eight-year-old cellist Pablo Casals. Beginning with the Roosevelts, elegant programs were printed, and concerts became a regularly scheduled part of White House life.[17]

During Roosevelt's administration, moreover, the donation of the first state concert grand piano to the White House by Steinway & Sons in 1903 established the East Room as a focal point for the performing arts.[18] Now the world's greatest pianists — Paderewski, Busoni, Hofmann, Rachmaninoff, Myra Hess, and that brilliant, fiery lady from San Antonio, Texas, Olga Samaroff (born Lucy Hickerlooper) — came to perform for the president, First Lady, and their distinguished guests. Steinway & Sons arranged most of the concerts held in the White House during the first half of the century. Significantly, the firm's correspondence with Edith Roosevelt indicates their mutual preference for American music and American artists at a time when our nation was still under the cultural thumb of Europe. When the great baritone from Philadelphia David Bispham sang "Danny Deever" to words by Rudyard Kipling, the song was so spirited that it brought the president to his feet shouting: "By Jove! That was bully! With such a song as that you could lead a nation into battle!"[19] Teddy Roosevelt often cried "Bully!" when Paderewski played, too. The only problem was that he could never wait until Paderewski had finished playing.

When one considers America's twentieth-century presidents and music, Harry S Truman and John F. Kennedy are the first who come to many people's minds. Ironically, these two dynamic leaders were enormously different in their musical interests. Truman was an ardent music lover and amateur pianist, but held only one season of musical programs in the White House in the eight years he was president. John F. Kennedy, by contrast, did not really care for music. Some who knew him well said it hurt his ears.[20] Yet the three short years of the Kennedy administration were filled with staged operas, concerts, ballet, youth concerts, and musical theater. Jacqueline Kennedy, who was knowledgeable in all the arts, claimed her main concern was to present the best and not necessarily what was popular at the time.[21] Thus, the Kennedys established the White House as a prominent center for America's artistic achievements. Their dedication and creativity provided a model for succeeding administrations to the present day.

In searching through the piles of music at the Truman Library in Independence, Missouri, one discovers that Chopin, Mozart, and Tchaikovsky outnumber the popular pieces, such as the famous "Missouri Waltz," which President Truman did not care for at all. But he was not at all shy about playing the piano and would play unabashedly for just about anyone. He played for world leaders (Stalin and Churchill); for U.S. presidents (John F. Kennedy); for concert artists (Eugene List); for movie stars (Jack Benny); for painters (Grandma Moses); and for some 30 million Americans during his televised tour of the newly remodeled White House. Perhaps, as he admitted, the fingers would not work on all the pieces he knew — but he would play them anyway. He was once asked if he sang tenor or baritone, and he replied: "I *never* sing. I'm saddest when I sing and so are those who listen to me."[22]

The traditions of early White House musical life were carried into the twentieth century by several presidents who deserve far more credit for their attention to American artistic values than we have given them. Calvin Coolidge and Herbert Hoover, for example, brought enough fine programs to the White House to rival Carnegie Hall. Vladimir Horowitz, Mary Garden, Rosa Ponselle, Jascha Heifetz, Maria Jeritza, John McCormack, Gregor Piatigorsky, and numerous other luminaries performed for the Hoovers. With the young harpist Mildred Dilling, who played for the king of Siam, Lou Henry Hoover began the tradition of inviting a guest artist to entertain a visiting head of state.

Under the administration of Franklin Roosevelt, however, a new era of White House history began. During the twelve years of the Franklin Roosevelt administration, more than three hundred concerts were held in the White House. These programs were indeed unique because they reached out to every corner of America. They seemed to reflect the president and First Lady's understanding of the communicative powers of music in an era of depression and war. To the White House came the power and pathos of black voices, the music of Native Americans, important women's musical organizations, and an array of folk singers close to the sea, soil, and heart of America.

The Roosevelts' eclectic tastes, however, resulted in some unusual juxtapositions. A fiery interpretation of a bullfight by the dancer La Argentina was followed by the Vienna Boys' Choir's serene interpretation of "Silent Night." On another occasion, Lawrence Tibbett, the Metropolitan Opera baritone, shared his program for the king and queen of England with the Coon Creek Girls, a square dance team.[23] Little did it matter; the royal couple loved it.

Before concluding this short musical tour of the White House, mention should be made of some of our other *unsung* presidents — Dwight Eisenhower, for one. Many of Eisenhower's White House concerts accented military ensembles, the fine "court" musicians of the mansion. But Eisenhower also brought Artur Rubinstein to the White House for his only appearance there. He also extended presidential patronage, for the first time, to that great, dynamic American art form — Broadway musical theater. Lyndon and Lady Bird Johnson enjoyed an extraordinary array of ballets and musical shows, many held on the White House lawn for hundreds of guests. The Nixons and Fords broadened their pro-

President and Mrs. Kennedy greet members of the American Ballet Theater after their performance at the White House. Courtesy of the John F. Kennedy Library.

grams to include a wider variety of American musical styles than ever before — jazz, country, gospel, and many other forms.

There were times, however, when not even the White House could escape the explosive musical messages of the 1960s and early 1970s. For we were a nation engulfed in unrest manifest in nearly every aspect of American life. On different occasions at the Johnson White House, singer Eartha Kitt and poet Robert Lowell lashed out unmercifully against the war in Vietnam, and Carol Feraci shocked the Nixons and their guests with an antiwar demonstration staged right in the middle of a song. But these were not the first times politics and music collided at the White House. One hundred years earlier, in the elegant Red Room, the legendary Hutchinson Family sang their songs of patriotism, abolition, and social injustice for President Abraham Lincoln, his family, and guests.

The White House, with its unique blending of music, politics, and protocol, has also been perennially prone to mishaps and infelicities of coordination. Once, the U.S. Marine Band struck up a rousing rendition of "The Lady Is a Tramp" just as the queen of England started to dance with President Ford. On another occasion, soprano Clamma Dale was rehearsing below the State Dining Room before her concert for the Carters and the premier of Romania. Just as President Carter lifted his glass and opened his mouth to begin after-dinner toasts, out came a brilliantly musical "ah-ah-ah-ah." Everybody looked around startled. The president tried again, and, as he opened his mouth to speak, out came the warm-up scales again. Someone ran quickly downstairs to warn Dale that she was standing at the base of the shaft going up to the fireplace directly behind the president. "For a moment," said the social secretary, Gretchen Poston, "we thought we had lost our soprano in a fireplace."[24]

Today television has brought us all closer to the White House because of the many concerts broadcast from the East Room. The Carters initiated the concept, opening with a program by Vladimir Horowitz in 1978. The Reagans and Bushes continued the practice with a special accent on American music and artists. Other musical traditions are also kept alive, such as the programs by guest artists for elegant state dinners, the social and ceremonial music played by the U.S. Marine Band and other military ensembles, the children's concerts, and music for

The 1978 White House Jazz Festival demonstrated the president's ability to showcase American talent and inform public taste. Here, President Carter's invited guests listen to ragtime pianist Eubie Blake on the South Lawn. During the nineteenth century, band concerts at an unfenced White House were open to all. Courtesy of the White House Historical Association.

parties on the White House lawn. "All," as Mrs. Bush relates, "have enriched life at the White House and are wonderfully representative of all that our American culture has to offer."[25]

Thus the ceremonial traditions, the pageantry associated with the presidency, still play as significant a role today as they did during the earliest decades of the presidency. In many ways they are even more vital. Through White House musical traditions, our spirits seem to cling to a bygone era, to an age of romantic chivalry in a time of burgeoning technology and commercialism. As Anatole Broyard, a critic with the *New York Times*, wrote: "In a sense, America was discovered because European romanticism had nowhere to go. It had exhausted its poetic impulse in chivalry, kings, castles, and cathedrals."[26]

Perhaps those words offer an explanation for that unique American phenomenon — White House music. Curiously, by the early twentieth century, our state musical traditions had become more visible and established as many of those in Europe declined. Certain practices that we borrowed from abroad, such as the "command performance" and the gala after-dinner state entertainment by famous artists, barely exist anymore in the major European countries. Have they been transferred to the New World, where they are enjoyed as lingering vestiges of romanticism? Might they be useful tools to gain support for the arts in a nation that lacks the extensive government subsidies found in Europe? Is the music of the White House a mere image, after all? Perhaps. But it is a lyric image, a joyous vision, and the most graceful language of glory the president will ever know.

Music will always be a vital part of the American adventure of discovery, and the White House will be a prime mover in the voyage. While administrations change, tastes shift, and new currents explore fresh artistic terrain, in this music the image of America remains, reinforcing our heritage and glorifying our dreams.

NOTES

1. For more on White House musical history, see Elise K. Kirk, *Musical Highlights from the White House* (Malabar, Fla.: Krieger, 1992) and its earlier edition, *Music at the White House: A History of the American Spirit* (Champaign: University of Illinois Press, 1986). The author's articles on this subject

appear in *The Magazine Antiques, Washington Opera Magazine, American Way, Prologue, Opera News, The New Grove Dictionary of American Music, The Harry S. Truman Encyclopedia,* and other publications. Concerts of White House music were presented during the White House bicentennial at the Corcoran Gallery of Art, February 2, 1992, and at Catholic University of America ("Great Performances from the White House") by the university symphony orchestra and distinguished soloists, October 19, 1992.

2. Daniel J. Boorstin, *The Americans: The National Experience* (New York: Random House, 1965).

3. David Morse, *American Romanticism,* 2 vols. (Totowa, N.J.: Barnes & Noble, 1987), 1:1.

4. Ibid., 2.

5. On June 30, 1789, Washington paid Thomas Dodds "16 Guineas, 4 Guineas being allowed for an old Spinnett." Stephen Decatur, Jr., *Private Affairs of George Washington from the Records and Accounts of Tobias Lear, Esquire, His Secretary* (Boston: Houghton Mifflin Co., 1933), 35.

6. Music performed at this reception probably included pieces listed in a handwritten document dated 1804 in the files of the United States Marine Band, Marine Corps Historical Center, Navy Yard, Washington, D.C. See also *National Intelligencer,* September 25, 1805.

7. Jefferson to Nathaniel Burwell, March 14, 1818, in Thomas Jefferson, *The Writings of Thomas Jefferson,* ed. Andrew A. Lipscomb and Albert Ellery Bergh, 20 vols. (Washington: Thomas Jefferson Memorial Association, 1904–1905), 15:135.

8. Account #29.494, Record Group 217, Miscellaneous Treasury Accounts for the President's House (1800–1867), Office of Public Buildings and Grounds, National Archives and Records Services. The voucher indicates that the music was "bot [*sic*] of Joseph Milligen" and delivered to Mrs. Madison on October 12, 1810. A copy of this collection of music (*Journal of Musick, Composed of Italian, French and English songs, romances and duetts, and of overtures, rondos, etc. for the Forte Piano,* Part I, 1810) is at the Library of Congress.

9. Ivor Forbes Guest, *Fanny Elssler* (London: Adam & Black, 1970), 136–38.

10. John Tasker Howard, *Our American Music* (New York: Crowell, 1946), 230. Howard quotes from *Shadows on the Wall* by John Hill Hewitt, a composer, who accompanied Heinrich to the White House.

11. Louis Moreau Gottschalk, *Notes of a Pianist,* ed. Clara Gottschalk Peterson (Philadelphia: J. B. Lippincott, 1881). See also Kirk, *Musical Highlights from the White House,* 103.

12. John Lair, *Songs Lincoln Loved* (New York: Duell, Sloan and Pearce, 1954), ix. See also Philip D. Jordan, "Some Lincoln and Civil War Songs," *Abraham Lincoln Quarterly* (September 1942). Favorites of Lincoln included Foster's

"Gentle Annie," Dempster's "The Lament of the Irish Immigrant," Bishop's "Home, Sweet Home," and Russell's "Ship on Fire."

13. *New York Herald,* February 21, 1861.

14. *National Republican,* October 17, 1862.

15. *National Republican,* November 14, 1878.

16. *Washington Weekly Star,* March 26 and June 11, 1886.

17. Records documenting White House musical events during the Theodore Roosevelt administration are housed at the National Archives (Record Group 42, Official White House Social Functions, Office of Public Buildings and Grounds). They comprise several scrapbooks of printed programs, guest lists, invitations, newspaper clippings, and miscellaneous memoranda, and are the earliest organized data for a study of White House musical history.

18. The piano was decorated with paintings of graceful female figures by the noted American artist Thomas Wilmer Dewing. It remained in the White House until Steinway replaced it in 1938 with a piano that is still there today. For more on Steinway's role in White House history, see the correspondence from this period through Eisenhower's administration in the archives of Steinway & Sons, New York City.

19. David Bispham, *A Quaker Singer's Recollections* (New York: Macmillan, 1920), 317.

20. August Heckscher, interview with Wolf von Eckhardt, December 10, 1965, transcript, Kennedy Papers, John F. Kennedy Library, Boston.

21. Jacqueline Kennedy Onassis, interview with author, February 3, 1984.

22. "Music and Art," p. 8 of a nine-page typed questionnaire, n.d. President's Personal Files, Truman Papers, Harry S Truman Library, Independence, Missouri.

23. Programs and related documentation for the FDR period are found at the Franklin Roosevelt Library, Hyde Park, N.Y., in President's Personal Files 100; Eleanor Roosevelt Papers 80.3, #986, and 80.9, #993, and other files.

24. Gretchen Poston, interview with author, July 7, 1981.

25. Anna Perez, letter to author, October 29, 1991.

26. Kirk, *Musical Highlights from the White House,* xvi.

Epilogue

A House Set
in a Landscape

David McCullough

On a morning in May 1804, there arrived at the President's House, by
Baltimore coach, an extraordinary young European, a geologist, geogra-
pher, botanist, linguist, and archaeologist, a university unto himself, as
the poet Goethe said of Alexander von Humboldt. He had come to see
the president of the United States because he was interested in what the
president, Thomas Jefferson, had written in his *Notes on Virginia* about
mastodon teeth. And young Humboldt, too, had some things to say
about mastodon teeth that he had recently uncovered in the Andes.

Humboldt arrived in Washington at the end of one of the most extraordinary expeditions of all time, an epic exploration of Latin America. He had explored the Orinoco to its sources. He had gone south over
the mountains and climbed Mount Chimborazo to an altitude of nineteen thousand feet, which was higher than anyone had ever gone at that
point, even in a balloon. All his great fame, the Humboldt Current, the
dozens of geological points in our own country that were to be named
for Alexander von Humboldt, were still in the future.

Humboldt was still unknown because most of his reputation would
come from the numerous books he would write as a result of this Latin
American adventure. But that in no way limited President Thomas Jefferson's interest. For days on end, the two of them could be seen walking
the White House grounds, deep in conversation, Humboldt shifting

back and forth from English to French to German to Spanish, seemingly unaware that he was even doing it. And apparently Jefferson had no difficulty keeping up with him.

The scene on the lawn, of these two extraordinary nineteenth-century men walking up and down, back and forth, talking science, talking ideas, talking geography, talking about the future, is one I would dearly love to have observed. Lewis and Clark had been sent to the Far West by Jefferson only the year before, in 1803, and Humboldt's expedition had far eclipsed that of Lewis and Clark both in its extent and in its findings.

Jefferson and Humboldt were birds of a feather, if there ever were, and, of course, the talk was of a kind rarely heard in Washington. Much of what goes on in life is talk, and, heaven knows, so is much of what has gone on at the White House. Talk, talk, talk. Much of what has transpired at the White House has been very pleasant, as on lovely mornings in May when two celebrated intellectual giants could meet and discuss what interested them the most. Christmas mornings, soirees, musicals, teas, all of that. But much of it, let us not forget, has been tragic in the extreme — death, great sorrow, madness, alcoholism, treachery, self-recrimination, agonized disappointment of a kind that none of us could possibly imagine. The awful strain of someone dying in the other room has happened at the White House many times. And the presence always, of course, of the past, the heavy, sometimes disturbing, often invigorating presence of our presidential past.

On a rain-soaked afternoon in April 1945, with Franklin Roosevelt lying in state in the East Room, the White House was filled with grief such as had been felt only at the time of Lincoln's death in another April. When Harry Truman entered the room, no one thought to stand up; no one was thinking then of the current president of the United States, only the dead president, and all that was ending with him.

Truman's own best friend, Charlie Ross, dropped dead in the West Wing of overwork. Ross was his press secretary, and I am sure that Truman felt — because of the kind human being he was — that he may have been partly responsible for working Charlie so hard, for not insisting that Charlie leave his job.

Truman's mother-in-law, Madge Gates, also died in the White House, in Truman's second term, upstairs in the room across the hall from the

president's. Moreover, Truman was convinced through most of his presidency, particularly up until the time the White House was rebuilt, that
the place was haunted — which added to its appeal, because of his fascination with his predecessors. John Quincy Adams, Andrew Jackson,
James K. Polk, Abraham Lincoln — they stirred an imagination that can
only be described as truly historical. Truman was in office only a short
time when he wrote one of several wonderful letters on the subject, this
to his wife, Bess, who was back home in Missouri.

Truman disliked using the telephone and loved to write letters, and,
as a consequence, thousands of his letters have survived. In one month
in 1947, for example, he wrote Bess twenty-two times. On June 12,
1945, two months to the day after he had taken office, he wrote her this
account:

> Just two months ago today, I was a reasonably happy and contented Vice
> President. Maybe you can remember that far back too. But things have
> changed so much, it hardly seems real. I sit here in this old house and
> work on foreign affairs, and read reports, and work on speeches — all the
> while listening to the ghosts walk up and down the hallway — and even
> right here in the study. The floors pop and the drapes move back and
> forth. I can just imagine Old Andy and Teddy having an argument over
> Franklin. Or James Buchanan and Franklin Pierce deciding which was
> more useless to the country. And when Millard Fillmore and Chester Ar-
> thur join in for place and show, the din is almost unbearable. . . .

It was because the old house was so decrepit — at least this is the interpretation you can take if you are of a literal frame of mind — that doors
would suddenly swing open of their own accord. The upstairs floors
would pop, groan, and moan through the night, and Truman, particularly when his wife was away, would get up and walk about by himself,
up and down the halls. He would look in his closets or wind the clocks.

Another time he wrote to her:

> Night before last I went to bed at nine o'clock after shutting my doors.
> At four o'clock I was awakened by three distinct knocks on my bedroom
> door. I jumped up and put on my bathrobe, opened the door, and no one
> was there. Went out and looked up and down the hall, looked into your
> room and Margie's. Still no one. Went back to bed after locking the doors,

and there were footsteps in your room whose door I'd left open. Jumped
up and looked and no one there! Damn place is haunted, sure as shootin'.

He then added another sentence that is extremely interesting: "Secret
Service said not even a watchman was up here at that hour." The president was there all by himself — with his ghosts.

His favorite cousin, Ethel Nolan, once said that for Harry history
wasn't something in a book — it was "part of life," an extension of life,
an enlargement of the human experience. When Truman spoke of those
presidents of the past, it was as if he were talking about people he knew.

Those of us who are interested in the White House look at old prints
and old photographs. We study architectural drawings, floor plans, en-
gineering diagrams, and scale models. We stand outside the iron fence
and peer in. We are nearly always looking at the White House from the
outside.

But what of those who look out from the inside? What is the view
from the other direction? For those who live in the White House?

Of utmost importance to any who write history or biography is the
capacity for empathy. To be able to put yourself in another person's
shoes, in another person's skin. What do the occupants of the White
House see, looking out?

Most obviously, immediately, you see you are in a landscape. You do
not seem to be in the city proper. The White House is not like 10 Downing Street, or the Élysée Palace. You are in a park. If you are standing in
the doorway of the Blue Room and face the north door, you are looking
into Lafayette Park, which is a visual extension of your own park setting. With the wonderful Andrew Jackson statue in view, you are reminded, if you are the president, that you are but one link in the long
chain of presidents reaching into the past. If you turn and look through
the window to the south, the vista opens wider still — to the green
sweep of the lawn, the ballpark, the Mall, and the Jefferson Memorial
beyond. And then to the Potomac, and all that the river suggests, of time
passing, of change, continuity, and the vast continent from which the
river flows. You are joined by the Potomac to the rest of America. These
are feelings all intended by Pierre-Charles L'Enfant, who planned the
city, and James Hoban, who designed the White House. From the house,

we see spring arrive; summer bear down; fall color the world outside; winter settle in. It is a setting to help one maintain a sense of proportion.

For Jefferson and Humboldt on their walks, the setting was a stimulant for conversation, a background suitable for talk of the mastodon teeth and God knows what else. Harry Truman built a famous balcony so he could better see the garden, enjoy the landscape, the view. One summer evening, taking his supper with Mrs. Truman out on the porch, observing that view, he was inspired to make an interesting observation on the human condition. This was recorded on a scrap of paper now in the Truman Library, one of many such "diary entries" that have survived in the president's hand:

> A ball game or two goes on in the park south of the lawn. Evidently a lot of competition, from the cheers and calls of the coaches. A robin hops around looking for worms, finds one and pulls with all his might to unearth him. A mocking bird imitates the robin, jays, redbirds, crows, hawks — but has no individual note of his own. A lot of people like that.

"Planes take off and land at National Airport south of Jefferson Memorial," Truman continues. "It is a lovely evening. . . ." In his imagination, he pictured the old Washington Canal crossing the grounds on the Washington Monument, as it had long ago. He saw the barges anchored somewhere west of the monument. "I can see old J. Q. Adams going swimming in it and getting his clothes stolen by an angry woman who wanted a job. Then I wake up, go upstairs and go back to work."

Historians may be as poor at predicting the future as anybody. But something we do know will continue. We will continue to be human beings. We will continue to need to be in touch with our past, to know who we are; and we will continue to need to be in touch with nature, to know who we are and to give a sense of proportion to our outlook. One of my favorite books is called *Spring Comes to Washington*, by Louis J. Halle, Jr. It places in such revealing juxtaposition the busy business of bureaucratic Washington and the timeless cycles of nature, comings and goings in this very place that have occurred over tens of thousands of years and will no doubt continue unless we make a worse mess of things. . . .

Theodore Roosevelt was a genius. Probably, with Lincoln and Jefferson, he was one of the three bona fide geniuses who have occupied the White House. One morning when Roosevelt was walking with his sister Corinne on the White House grounds, walking, talking, talking, as he always did, he stopped and picked up between his forefinger and his thumb a tiny feather. Looking at it, he said, "Very early for a fox sparrow." Consider what that says about his sense of proportion.

Often, reading about the Civil War, I wonder how decent, well-meaning, church-going men and women, people who loved their families, loved their children and their country, could have been slaveholders. How could they have owned human beings? How was it possible that they didn't see how wrong that was? And then I wonder, what are we doing today that will lead others someday to ask the same of us? How could they have been so blind? How could they have been so selfish and stupid about the environment? Didn't they see what they were doing, and how wrong it was?

Alexander von Humboldt was the father of ecology, as we now call it. In his explorations in the Andes, he saw that different kinds of plants grew at different altitudes, and he brought back both plant and soil specimens and began to postulate new theories. Let us hope that in the future we will have presidents who will want the Alexander von Humboldts of tomorrow to call on the White House. Let us hope that future presidents of the United States will have enough humanity to find in nature reflections on the human condition, as did President Truman. And let us hope we will have presidents of the United States who have both the time and curiosity to stop for a look at a sparrow feather.

We have gathered here for this conference from twenty-one states. We are architects and engineers and historians. We work for the National Park Service. At least a dozen have worked at the White House or now serve on the staff. Several are leading presidential historians and biographers. And here we all are. And why? Why do we care?

I think we are subject to the pull of the past, perhaps more than most others. And I think what pulls us to the past is not that it is something static, but that it is something fluid. The essence of history is change. Everything is always changing, and the more dramatic and fascinating the change — whether it is a change in events or a change in the cast on a stage — the more we are drawn to it, and the more we see our lives being enlarged by the experience. There is absolutely no reason why any literate human being has to be provincial in time, any more than in space. Why would we wish to cut ourselves off from the vast experience that precedes us, which is so much larger than anything we can possibly know in the brief time we are allotted on earth?

We are also drawn to the past because it is a good story. And when we think about all that has happened, say in a house such as the White House, we are drawn in irresistibly. I think, too, that we are here because we love the White House and primarily because we love our country.

N O T E

The story of Alexander von Humboldt's visit to Washington is told in Charles C. Sellers, *Charles Willson Peale: Later Life, 1790–1827* (Philadelphia: American Philosophical Society, 1947), 182–84. The correspondence of Jefferson and Humboldt is in the *Proceedings of the American Philosophical Society* 103 (December 1959): 787–95. Interested readers might also wish to consult Daniel J. Boorstin, *The Lost World of Thomas Jefferson* (Boston: Beacon Press, 1948). David McCullough has written biographies of Theodore Roosevelt and Harry S Truman: *Mornings on Horseback* (New York: Simon & Schuster, 1981) and *Truman* (New York: Simon & Schuster, 1992). Robert H. Ferrell has edited *Dear Bess: The Letters of Harry to Bess Truman* (New York: W. W. Norton & Co., 1983) and *The Autobiography of Harry S. Truman* (Boulder: Colorado Associated University Presses, 1980). He has also written *Harry S. Truman and the Modern American Presidency* (Boston: Little, Brown & Co., 1983). John Hersey's interesting "Mr. President: Ghosts in the White House," was published in *The New Yorker* 27 (April 28, 1951): 36–55.

Bibliographical Note

William Seale, *The President's House,* 2 vols. (Washington: White House Historical Association, 1986), is a magnificent scholarly history of the building and its changing uses throughout American history. *The White House: An Historical Guide* (Washington: White House Historical Association, 1991) updates the 1961 guide and is a short, illustrated, accessible work. James Sterling Young, *The Washington Community: 1800–1828* (New York: Columbia University Press, 1966), and Constance McLaughlin Green, *Washington: Capital City, 1789–1950* (Princeton, N.J.: Princeton University Press, 1962), are excellent at placing the White House and the presidency in the context of the government and city surrounding them.

Aside from biographies and memoirs of presidents, First Ladies, and public officials, the following general works shed light on the White House and the presidency: Robert H. Ferrell, *Ill-Advised: Presidential Health and Public Trust* (Columbia: University of Missouri Press, 1992); Richard G. Hutcheson, *God in the White House: How Religion Has Changed the Modern Presidency* (New York: Macmillan, 1988); Edmund Fuller and David E. Green, *God in the White House: The Faiths of American Presidents* (New York: Crown, 1968); William O. Stoddard, *Inside the White House in War Times* (New York: C. L. Webster, 1890); Richard Norton Smith and Timothy Walch, eds., *Farewell to the Chief: Former Presidents in American Public Life* (Worland, Wyo.: High Plains Publishing Co., 1990); Tim R. Blessing and Robert K. Murray, *Greatness in the White House: Rating the Presidents Washington through Carter*

(University Park: Pennsylvania State University Press, 1988); Paul Boller, *Presidential Anecdotes* (New York: Oxford University Press, 1981); and Elizabeth Frost, ed., *The Bully Pulpit: Quotations from America's Presidents* (New York: Facts on File, 1988).

Index

211